Dave Anthony's Moods:

Dave Anthony's Moods:

This Obscure Group

A personal memoir of the best unheard band of the Sixties.

Tim Large

Copyright © Tim Large 2015

Published in 2015 by YouCaxton Publications

ISBN 978-1-909644-939

All rights reserved. No part of this publication may be reproduced, stored in a retrieval system or transmitted in any form, or by any means, without the prior written permission of the holder of the copyright, nor be otherwise circulated in any form, binding or cover other than that in which it is published and without a similar condition being imposed on the subsequent purchaser.

My thanks to:

Those surviving members of the band who provided me with a lot of extra information, confirmation and, sometimes, correction. Bob, Bill, Andy, Chris, Bob, thanks guys.

My family and friends for their unflagging encouragement.

Special thanks to Luca Selvini, an Italian enthusiast of Sixties music, who curates a marvellous Facebook page about Dave Anthony's Moods and has co-authored his own exhaustive history of the band (which I must own to not having fully read. I promise to read the English translation!)

Apart from those specifically acknowledged, all the photographs are either from Luca's collection, reproduced with his permission, or are my own.

To Richard

Preface

Some time ago, wandering around the internet in a vague search for my past, I stumbled on a site called *Vinyl Vultures*. Someone had posted an item about a record they'd come across, called *Talking to the Rain* by Dave Anthony's Moods, with a comment "does anyone know anything about this obscure group?" I thought I did, so I posted some replies.

Rapidly, a small volcano of interest, information, facts and lies exploded, across Britain and the rest of Europe.

I thought: somebody should write this down, and I'm the only one who can.

As it says at the top, this is going to be a personal memoir, as much about me as about the group. Don't expect scandalous revelations or insights. I'm just going to write it down as I remember it, from where I see it now. There will be fuzzy recollections, big blanks in the factual scheme, biased slants for which the libelled persons could probably sue me or my estate – I don't care about any of that. What you read is all you get from me.

• • •

The version of *Talking to the Rain* posted on Vinyl Vultures turned to be the demo from which we made the record, rather than our reinterpretation. I dug out my scratchy original DAM 45, played it, listened carefully to it, and remembered where, when and how it was made. Then I started to write this.

How I Got Music

I first became aware of my musical talent quite late on. I had heard, loved, and even listened to music ever since my ears opened (my father singing me to sleep with *A Long Way to Tipperary* and *Pack Up Your Troubles* and *My Grandfather's Clock*; I think those songs will be my last memory traces to erase themselves). I knew as well, from early on, that it was made by human beings. My mother could play the piano, and her father the violin. But it took me a long time to realise that I too might be like that.

Bournemouth in the post-war years, before the end of rationing, must have been a dull place, although I wouldn't have known that. We lived in Southbourne. From the cliffs, the vista was defined by Hengistbury Head, then the distant Isle of Wight (the Polar Bear) to the left, Old Harry Rocks with the lights of Swanage beyond, on a clear night, twenty miles to the right, and in between, the vast expanse of blue or lead pencil grey or silver sea, and the endless horizon. The cliffs, the beach with its alarmingly seasonal changes of sand levels, the charcoal tarmac prom, the barnacle-crusted seaweed-tangled breakwaters, the icy finger-whitening water. Once the barbed wire had been cleared from the beach (placed there just in case Hitler decided that Bournemouth was going to be one of his Normandy beaches;

both piers were blown up for similar reasons: we weren't going to let him dock his pleasure-boats here either, were we?), the family beach-hut was quickly salvaged, painted and reinstated by my energetic father, who had doubtless learned this principle of continual recovery, repair and restitution from his years in the Merchant Navy between the wars. I guess that was also where he learned the songs. Certainly he never showed any other signs of musicality.

He was away for most of the war, in Malvern and other places, on important scientific business which the family believed to have been to do with the development of radar, though he never talked about it, having presumably signed the Official Secrets Act. Come to think of it, he never talked about anything much until his very late years, preferring to retreat to his workshop, where he mended things, did obscure works of electronics, and crafted exquisite pieces of woodwork and furniture. But on home visits, he sang me to sleep with those songs, I think, before I could walk properly. There were others – *Waltzing Matilda*, *My Darling Clementine*, even Lead Belly's *Good Night Irene* – these melodies and lyrical stories plunged into my psyche at a very early age. I remember his pride in me when he came back on a visit and I had mastered the use of a wheelbarrow (I was four); at six, I helped him shift the sand from the road to the back garden when he single-handedly built the new garage at the side of 37 (which still stands). After he came home for good, he never sang to me again. But I can still hear his light tenor voice, or so I imagine. Maybe I even sang along, though I doubt it, except perhaps in my head.

Inland, Southbourne was actually a bit drab. From our house at 37 Watcombe Road my horizons were limited, compared to the exotic glories of Bournemouth and the western reaches of

Canford Cliffs and Sandbanks. I learnt to walk to Southbourne Prep School on my own (being bullied by rougher boys like the Dodwells), to make my way to the playing fields at the end of Leigham Vale Road, and to the paper shop and the 'Polliwog' in Kimberley Road, for the Eagle and sweets. We were taken out for drives, where we admired the likes of Jack Hawkins or Mantovani's house in Glenfurness Avenue from afar; but Southbourne wasn't anything like that. My parents were quite well-off professionals, as were most of their friends and neighbours, but I think I was aware from very early times that life within these, the only boundaries I could discern or imagine, wasn't going to be particularly exciting. Exciting was something that happened elsewhere, out in the mysterious world of 'Picture Post' and 'Illustrated' magazines, The Children's Encyclopaedia, the weird programmes my parents religiously tuned in to on the wireless – ITMA, the Billy Cotton Band Show (this wasn't really about music, despite its title; more of a comedy show. We held our breath for the catchphrases and the novelty numbers; I can still do the tune, though not the words, of *Two Little Men in a Flying Saucer*. I'm not particularly proud of this.) and Music While You Work (definitely a music programme! My love of military marches stems from there.)

Though I'd woken up to it, discovered that it was actually made by people rather than just dropped in on us from some higher place, actual occurrence in my ears of this music stuff was haphazard, because I had no direct access. My parents controlled the radio. When we moved from 37 Watcombe to 3 Stourwood Road when I was twelve, though, my grandparents moved with us, and with them my grandfather's record collection and radiogram. Previously, there had been musical events (later we'd call them 'record sessions') at 66 Watcombe, where my pleasantly pissed grandfather would impose *Phil the Fluter's Ball*, *William Tell* and the *1812*, 10 and 12 inch 78s, on an audience of several increasingly embarrassed adult relatives, and one enthralled grandson. I think Grandpa was what they call a 'character'. At 66 Watcombe he kept chickens and grew raspberries. When I found a grub in one of the latter, plucked off the cane, he advised me solemnly that meat was rationed and I should count myself lucky. In his late sixties, in about 1952, he suffered a significant stroke which left him almost blind and bedridden, as a result of which the great family decision to move must have been taken. Our lovely, gentle, worn-out Grannie was dragged along behind this.

So, the move to 3 Stourwood Road in 1954 was the result of grown-up decisions to pool and exploit resources to provide a more manageable care regime for my grandfather. I think my parents must also have received some kind of income or capital boost at this time. Certainly, they pulled in some funds from selling the old Stamford Road house which they had kept, and let, when they bought 37 Watcombe before the War. They had to go to law to evict the evil black-snaggle-toothed witch who rented it.

Of course, at the time I was only vaguely aware of this grown-up stuff. I was only vaguely aware of my own existence – I was too busy sorting out the chaos that was incessantly blasting in through my eyes, my fingers with their chilblains, my runny nose, and most of all, my ears. At six, I was scared, panicked by loud noises: a train letting off steam, the huge presses at the laundry which hissed like demented snakes, any big unexpected bangs – all this kind of unsolicited sound was a threat against my efforts to convert the randomness of this invasive aural chaos into some kind of order, something more like music. By twelve,

I'd overcome those panics, but still it took me some years to understand that music can be built, in your head, out of pretty much anything, that the order is within you, silently waiting to impose itself on the chaos.

Much more importantly, the move enabled the control and exploitation of musical resources. There was a room at the back of the house, beyond the kitchen and the pantry, originally (my father wryly suggested) the maid's quarters. It immediately became the Den (from 'Life With The Lyons', a popular radio half-hour comedy series of the time), and the exclusive territory of us three kids and our musical resources – Grandpa's monolithic oaken radiogram with its fret-worked loudspeaker grill; huge piles of 78s of all diameters, inherited and later acquired; and constantly replenished supplies of gramophone needles. We spent hours sifting through those mysterious, fragile black circles, with their spiral groove etched into their surface in their brown paper sleeves, randomly prospecting for aural gold. A record would be put on, briefly assessed, then rejected. Or, occasionally, set aside into the pile that needed revisiting. Perhaps one in twenty would make it all the way through to the 'Favourites', then to be played to destruction forever, or at least for a week.

Later, once I understood the principle of the technology – that the most complex sound could be reduced to a single wave-form (play that back please: the 1812 Overture, played by a full 42 piece orchestra, boiled down to this one squiggly line, which could then be squiggle-etched into a spiralling groove on a chunk of shellac, and then converted, squiggled back, into the original symphony orchestra sound, or something approaching it, playing Tchaikovsky via a tiny needle and some mysterious electrics), then I spent hours closely studying those grooves, stupidly trying to decipher them, for all the world as if you could work back from the effect to the cause.

I'd love to know what those favourites were. But remember, we're dealing with incipient teenagers here – the memory of that process wipes out the detail. Of course, as well as the radiogram (which was only ever used as a gram, never as a radio), the heavy Sunday lunchtime stodge pudding of 'Two Way Family Favourites' on the Light Programme (Mario Lanza, Anne Shelton, Eve Boswell) must somehow have grown within me into a huge lump of my musical viscera. 'Children's Favourites' was another. I may kill myself next time *I'm a Pink Toothbrush* or *The Happy Wanderer* slides uninvited into my ears. But, there were some goodies even in those arid swamps, or soggy deserts. Even now, I wouldn't mind listening attentively to *Sparky's Magic Piano*. And I adored *The Drinking Song*.

Even before rock and roll, though, there was one huge breakthrough: we were allowed to save up and buy our own records! The significance of this can't be overstated. Suddenly, music wasn't just something that was done to you: you could, within the restrictive boundaries of parental approval and cash, exercise some control, get, in that instant, what you wanted, needed.

How did we know, in the instant, what we wanted? What told us so undeniably what we needed? There must have some very special force at play. Because, back in those 78rpm days, we couldn't be selective – we had nothing to select from. But somehow we did. *Chain Gang* by Jimmy Young (don't scoff, give it a listen; one of the earliest sound- rather than song-based productions), *Sixteen Tons* by Tennessee Ernie Ford, *Kisses Sweeter than Wine* by Jimmie Rodgers. I have no idea how, but I knew I had to get *Zambezi* (by Lou Busch on the purple-centred

Capitol label), rush it home and play this fragile 78 rpm single spiral over and over again on the radiogram.

Thus began my love affair with records. They combined so much art within the single artefact: the simple physical beauty of that perfect disc, with its cryptic centre label which seemed to hold depths of arcane information (what was 'ffrr'? what was the Capitol Tower? what did all those strange numbers mean?), the music it magically contained; and, dimly, the notion that perhaps here was a new art form in which sounds with no counterpart anywhere else could be contrived, constructed and preserved, like pieces of sculpture, within that black shiny squiggly ineluctable groove.

I was given piano lessons, by Mrs Smith. I hated them. It was all about technique and syntax – how to cross your fingers over to play a scale, how to read the different dots in the different clefs – nothing to do with what was going on in my ears. I dug my heels in and refused. Once this had been accepted, I was free to plonk around on my mum's Steinway upright and, sometime later, do a skeletal Jerry Lee Lewis impersonation (part of the solo in *You Win Again* to be exact). But Mrs Smith inadvertently taught me quite a lot, about scales, the difference between major and minor (a flattened third), and how chords grow out of scales, and harmonies grow out of both chords and scales. She had, of course, no idea that she was doing this, releasing my two innate gifts, musical instinct and analytical skill; but hey, belated thanks anyway, Mrs Smith.

I don't think she fully grasped the fourth element of music – rhythm! And she certainly didn't get the one that underpins them all, emotion; but I suppose that's beyond a teacher of technique's terms of reference. I got it, though.

And then, suddenly, it was 1956. The 7 inch 45 was invented and we had to have, and got, our green and beige Ferguson record player with the lovely cream and maroon 4-speed Collaro ten-disc auto-changer (the Dansette having been scathingly rejected). You could stack up ten 45s (your current top ten) – then as the last one drops onto the pile, you take off the arm which holds the stack in place, and the top record plays over and over until you choose to stop it. Brilliant! The records themselves were designed for this purpose, with serrations around the outer edge of the label to stop them skidding or damaging each other as they landed like a disciplined squadron of flying saucers.

Naturally, I – my elder sister having moved on to other interests and my younger brother not old enough to possess spending cash – I had to own more than ten 45s. Every penny of pocket money's worth of 45s. The exact chronology, obviously, is available elsewhere; by now, you'd expect it to have turned into one amorphous blur, and to some extent it has, but I like to recall two overlapping phases. First there was Bill Haley, with a few imitators like Freddie Bell and the Bellboys. This was exciting, although still rooted in the dance-band jazz/swing I'd grown up with – the explosive rim-shots, slapped bass, tuneless sax solos and of course Franny Beecher's vehement percussive guitar stabs, these added an edge to what was, essentially, old-fashioned stuff. Little Richard and Fats Domino crept in alongside, like aliens. And then Elvis came and hit us straight in the ears, guts and seething hormones. The rest followed. My enduring, confused memory of *Heartbreak Hotel* is hearing it late at night on some kind of radio in our holiday home in Pembrokeshire, presented by my sister as a secret thing that parents had to be protected from, weren't permitted to share. It was dark, mysterious, unattainable, addictive.

Meanwhile, in what I now see as yet another separate musical universe, skiffle had arrived. Me and my mates suddenly became aware, along with most of the male teenage population of Bournemouth if not England, that it was actually possible for human beings like us to do this stuff. You could hear how it worked. This had never occurred to us until we heard Lonnie Donegan, Johnnie Duncan and the Blue Grass Boys, the Vipers, Nancy Whiskey. So skiffle groups erupted all over the place.

Mike Caddy, Tony Barney and Pete Jennions were those leading, unshy boys who naturally formed skiffle groups. I was given the washboard, and begged my mother for thimbles. (The washboard itself was acquired from a long gone ironmongers' in Southbourne Grove. I have a washboard out in the garage, as it happens. Not the original one; I'd give it a try, but I only have one thimble). But soon after I'd been issued with it, and the other guys had bullied guitars out of their parents, frustration started to set in. I'd watch and listen to my friends painfully putting their fingers where the chord book said, strumming their dull strings, trying for the next chord from the sheet music, smugly flaunting their superiority. One boy worked out, and wrote down, lists of all the notes that fitted with each chord, so as to be able to play solos. (To be fair to him, this sounds in retrospect remarkably akin to the kind of analysis people like Miles, Bird, George Russell had been doing not that long ago, on another planet – but it helps if you have musical talent to begin with. Also if you allow more than just the major scale into the calculations.)

Frustration took over and forced the pace. "I can do that", I thought. My parents, I suppose recognising that my obsession must have had something behind it at least to be recognised, if not nurtured, got me a guitar.

The first thing I found out, once having discovered how to tune the thing, was that if you played the bottom three strings in succession, they spelled out the first three notes of *When I Fall In Love* (E, A, D). So I hunted around the keyboard and strings until I found the fourth note (C#), then the whole tune. I got a chord book and learned, in about three weeks, how to play four string majors, and join them together into as near as I could approach to what I was hearing on those relatively accessible skiffle records. (The rock'n'roll was way beyond our reach at this stage; how could anyone reproduce a sound like *All Shook Up* or *Hound Dog*?)

The guitar was a fairly decent blonde-topped round hole acoustic, with a black scratch-plate and a very high action, bought from Don Strike in Westbourne Arcade. I think I became leader of the pack when I demonstrated to the others (having waited for the blood blisters on my fingertips to subside a bit) the intro to *Last Train to San Fernando* – a dramatic chromatic chord riff, G, E, F, F#, G, *accelerando*, played with six string barré chords!

We'd get together after (or sometimes at) school and rehearse whatever Lonnie Donegan or Vipers number we'd decided interested us, teasing out the chord sequences, the words, the guitar parts; then early on summer evenings we'd go up to the shelters on the Southbourne cliffs and entertain the passing schoolmates, girls if lucky, more usually old people (some of whom I think loved it). *Bury My Body*, an early Lonnie Donegan number, hugely influenced me, with its bluesy changes and hammer-on guitar licks. Tony Barney had a five-string banjo, on which he could improvise, and I strongly remember a particular session (the skiffle group Sunday morning practice) which might just have been my first experience of the process later called 'jamming'. And the gut emotions that came with it.

But it wasn't going to last. Skiffle was being eased out by rock'n'roll. Music itself was turning back from a process into an experience, was becoming more like a kind of ether through which the barely detectable waves of everyone's hesitant reaching out rippled towards other people. Especially girls.

. . .

Record Sessions became central to my life, our lives. Girls could attend record sessions, whereas they were allowed nowhere near skiffle groups. Music became a tool of competition, a male display token: the more obscure, the more likely. I failed dismally at that game, my problem being that I couldn't merge together my interest in the music with my interest in the girls. At a record session, whilst others were manoeuvring, I was listening, analysing, trying to understand and remember what I was hearing. Girls could be dealt with elsewhere, and were – at Church on Sundays (a good social rendezvous), at the associated Youth Club in the All Saints Church Hall, with its ping-pong and fake curate-led record sessions (which were nothing like the real darkened-room thing); and at occasional lucky snogging sessions, even the odd unhooked bra, after dark, in the shelters on the Southbourne cliffs.

And then *Jailhouse Rock* came out, in January 58. For some reason, this record was a turning point, maybe because it was one of Elvis's first releases to feature an understandable, playable guitar riff, E F (bang bang) E F (bang bang), and not to feature too much inaccessible piano stuff like *All Shook Up*. Anyway, shortly afterwards Mike and Pete announced that skiffle was dead, so we had to play rock'n'roll. They were right. But to my astonishment, I was appointed as lead singer and lead guitarist. This may have been to do with my having mastered, after another finger-bleeding session on the acoustic, the intro to *That'll be the Day*. Also, according to Mike, "Tim's got the voice for it" – a mystery to this day.

Thus began an era of who knows how many short-lived groups, drawn from a school- and Southbourne-based pool of teenage enthusiasts. They came together, practised, squabbled about the music, in the quicksand of male 17 year old alliances and girls; broke up; regrouped in ever shifting configurations of the same six or eight people. I was usually in there. At some point, I acquired an electric guitar – a lovely turquoise semi-acoustic of unknown breed (but never, as far as I can recall, an amp, someone else must've had one).

All these groupings had two things in common: no drummers, and no gigs. The first was inevitable, given the price of drum kits and the obvious parental reaction should anyone dare to express any inclination in that direction. The second just didn't matter.

La Fiesta was where the youth of Southbourne went whenever they were allowed. Through the blur of the years, it seems that it was every single night, which obviously can't be true – we were only seventeen – but I know for sure that I went up there whenever I could. It was the only place to be.

La Fiesta was a tiny, narrow half-unit coffee bar up the Grove, the shape of which was uniquely suited to crammed bunches of teenagers, less interested in coffee than in each other. Go and have a look. It's now a nail bar (whatever one of those might be), but the shape of the place survives, and a bit of imagination will give you a feel for how the narrow wedge-shaped front window end, and the consequent shifting seatings and their consequent shifting allegiances, evolved from Saturday to Saturday and ruled our emotions. Harry, the owner, was a bit older than us, into jazz or its close relatives, and he encouraged us, I think, towards the many directions we kids were hesitantly exploring. Not least, philosophical ones. Robin Armstrong-Brown once put me down, because I'd failed to pick up on some vacuous clever sophistry of his, with the words "but, of course, you're not an intellectual are you?", which made me smart for some weeks. But he did bring his guitar, and performed skilled versions of Tom Lehrer songs, which opened up hitherto unexplored lyrical directions (except for Flanders and Swann, a gentler, earlier equivalent perhaps).

I got a Saturday night job washing up, soon graduating to waiting tables and operating the Gaggia, and so became a minor local celebrity, confident and popular (though it could sometimes be a bit of a drag to see the gang taking off to places unknown at eight o'clock then returning at eleven, well tanked, whilst I'd been tending the empty tables with only the company of Harry and Sue, the other regular staffer). But there was philosophical exploration in behind there. Harry said, in one of those conversations during the lull, "of course, nobody over twenty-five believes in conscience, do they?" You had to think about that.

School was something you needed to do between visits to La Fiesta, or sometimes adventurous trips on the 21 bus to Bournemouth, with the dangerous exotica of El Cabala or wanderings through the Lower Pleasure Gardens (the joke's an old Bournemouth one which I trust I don't need to repeat here – Al Stewart, I seem to recall, put it into a song) down to the Pier, under which, even then, enticingly strange creatures called 'beatniks' crouched and smoked.

By 1959, school was an irrelevance. Of course, I didn't in any way realise this or take it into my life – there was far too much chaos there already for me to consider alternatives to the preordained course I had been launched upon. Setting a pattern which would stay with me for decades, at school I just did what I had to in order to meet expectations, impatiently chopping my way through this routine to reach the parts that really mattered.

Thus the mid fifties blurred through into the late fifties. Time started to go faster. Elvis joined the army – we frowned and sniffed and felt betrayed and loyal at the same time, perhaps our first inkling of the complexity of grown-up emotions. Buddy and Eddie died. Rock'n'roll gradually lost, or had stolen, its innocence. Now, I'd say that what it actually lost was its innocent purism – and that this was indeed part of our growing up. Growing up consists, amongst other things, of the beginnings of an acceptance that the world, and your life in it, isn't just the pure, simple oneness of *That's Alright Mama*, but needs also to encompass Freddy Cannon and Fabian and *Because They're Young* and Ricky Nelson's more cringe-making slush (heroes would've crumbled into dust, melted into sludge had I allowed them to), and heartbreakingly sneaky behaviour by previously unconditionally loved girls. Being me, I lapped it all up, swallowed it whole and trotted, head down, towards the next revelation.

• • •

In October 1960, I went to Leeds University to study Economics. Consider, and put in context, the import of that sentence. I could cover the next three years as bullet points. I'd been slotted into the 'Economics' stream at school for A levels, simply because I didn't seem to fit into the other two: 'Science' or 'Arts'. Education in the fifties was like that.

I realised early on that Economics and I were not going to get on. We reached an uneasy truce – I would do the minimum necessary work to attain some kind of degree, and Economics would permit me to pursue other avenues. This is more or less what happened. I'm sure I was indulged by my professors and tutors. They might have thought they'd recognised one of the unclassifiables: shame they didn't know what to do with such a creature, or my life would have been very different. Or perhaps not a shame. I learnt a lot about pretty well everything except Economics during the fragile, insulated bubble of those three strangely self-contained years.

During my University vacations, we'd have desultory 'practice' sessions, the usual bunch (I think we actually found someone with a drum kit at one point, who unfortunately wasn't a drummer) trying to be Dion and the Belmonts or something. I'd get together with my mate Clem and unpick Everly Brothers parts (I was usually Phil). I can still do some of them today – I learnt a lot about harmony and counterpoint from deconstructing the Evs. The melodic lines cross over each other, so that, at their best, you can't tell what's the tune.

But it was three years of academic apathy, intellectual dilettantism, and musical stand-still. And, of course, beer and girls. In June 63 I took my finals, and to my astonishment achieved a degree, a third, the system's grudging recognition of talent unmatched by hard graft. Later, I learned that this was mainly due to my Essay paper, which Professor Maurice Beresford described to me as 'the best he had ever seen', and which was apparently used as an exemplar for future generations of students. (He wouldn't give me a copy though.) So all that mugging up on Bergson, Sartre, Camus, Dostoevsky, Chomsky and the rest came good in the end. I think I even managed to work a bit of Economics in there.

Andy Jenkinson and I had entered into a pact whereby, if we both failed, we'd take off and backpack round the world. As it was, he got a first. So it was back to Southbourne.

How Music Got Me

I became aware of the Beatles quite late on. *Love Me Do* came out in October 62, and briefly charted. If I heard it at all, I probably wrote it off as a discountable Bruce Channell copy (which it was). The closing down of my life in Leeds, the closing down of my university career, of tenuous or endurable friendships and red hot or chilly loves, the strange sense of loss – music had to wait in the queue once again, for a while. Even though I've painted my Leeds years as being a bit arid, I can now read between the lines and see that a head was building up, not just in me but everywhere.

When I got back to Southbourne in June, though, Beatles were everywhere, and so was a music explosion in which my brother, not having been stranded in the vile frozen North for three years, was well ahead of me. Beatles themselves aside, there was an effervescent secondary scene – Dylan, post-Belmonts Dion, Chuck Berry (totally missed first time round), early Spector, Howlin' Wolf, Jimmy Reed, Buffie St Marie, many many others. Thanks, Dick! During those brief speeding three or four months, you unwittingly drew me back from the pinhead-balancing angel act I'd been performing for three years – years that I saw much later were both an education and a lesson, but just then, in June 1963, seemed to have been a waste – you drew me back to music: which gleefully grabbed me, shook me up, spun me around till I was dizzy, and tipped me out. Naturally, being the elder brother, I rapidly purloined all these new musical influences and claimed them as my own, within the re-formed music-based circle I half-wittingly, half accidentally constructed and re-entered during that strange suspended summer of 1963.

For some time – until my parents gently reminded me that I was now meant to be one of the top 0.001% or whatever of the population of my age, and was therefore expected to become some kind of captain of industry, and therefore needed to get some kind of job, at least as a start point – I just bummed around.

It was great. I went to the beach – sometimes the far end of Southbourne towards Hengistbury Head (on my towel, alone, writing the first chapters of novels), other times around Boscombe or Bournemouth Pier; occasionally on car trips (having passed my test and annexed my mother's side-valve 850cc red leather seated Morris Minor for my own use) to Shell Bay, across the Sandbanks ferry, where whole days could be easily, indolently wasted on beach life. June and July and a bit of August 1963 slipped away.

It couldn't last. Among the many reasons for this, money was top of the list. I applied for, was interviewed for, and was rejected for, several captain of industry jobs. A particular one I remember, somewhere in the Midlands, made me sit a three hour economics degree-level exam paper, which I devastatingly failed. (I'd confidently assert that I've outlived the enterprise, and the people, that subjected me to this – but

I still recall the unpleasantness of the process.) Eventually, I got a job on the buses.

As 63 slid towards 64, I was happy to be confused and disorientated. The reversion from Leeds to Southbourne, from pubs, pot-holing, philosophy, free-wheeling, back to the La Fiesta world I'd left behind three years before – not to mention my parents' assumption that nothing had changed – I don't think it even occurred to them to reset their expectations of my behaviour – I just went into a kind of reactive trance, 'yes' to any question. This too was great. In between shifts on the buses, I surfed on the surface of my life. I was earning quite good money, kept at home and able to support myself in beer and fags; I bounced in and out of relationships (with far more sex than I'd ever imagined possible): and gradually, the idea of making music crept back in.

• • •

Bob Michaels had never been a great friend of mine until then (I was much closer to his older brother Terry). Suddenly, somehow though, Bob became my best mate – my pub-crawling, girl-hunting, music-jamming partner. He was a talented, proficient pianist whose tastes just about overlapped with mine at the margins. His heroes were mostly jazz, mostly pianists, and mostly Art Tatum. He had little time for pop, but was prepared to be dragged along in my musical wake. At first, we jammed at his house in Southbourne, just the two of us. By now, I'd somehow acquired a new red semi-acoustic Framus Fret Jet – as the name implies, a fabulously low action that enabled me to fake all sorts of stuff. God knows what we thought we were doing. When I try to think back there, I can only come up with a kind of parallel universe analogy. The music I was listening to and the music I was trying to play co-existed, but not only was there little if any common ground, it seems I was unaware of this split. I'd unknowingly shift, within the space of a ten minute walk, from some sort of folk-jazz improvisation loosely based on Monk and Coltrane (at Bob's) to *My Boyfriend's Back* by the Angels (at home). Neither of these two worlds was in any way simple.

Sometime before this, Harry had sold La Fiesta to an old queen called Reg. Reg made it clear from the outset that he was more interested in the afternoon old ladies than the evening youth trade, thereby killing this break-even youth culture venue stone dead (I think Reg's La Fiesta lasted eighteen months, if that). So we had to look further afield for our night-time adventures. Pubs were naturally important but couldn't be afforded every night, at least not all evening. Bob and I picked up on a kind of Christian youth club off the Old Christchurch Road, called the Wheelhouse. It was run by a big-bearded, low-key non-evangelistic music enthusiast called, I think, Terry. It was a place you could turn up at any time, rent a cup of coffee, buy a cheese roll and feed the well stocked juke-box. It was also frequented by local thugs, with whom I had at least two inadvertent run-ins due to my accidentally nicking, or being nicked by, their girl-friends.

The Wheelhouse also had, amazingly, a big hall with a stage, and Terry rented this facility out every so often, at cost, to local groups who were competing in the Beatle-fuelled maelstrom of musical aspiration. Problem was, Bob and I didn't actually have a group. Undiscouraged by this point of detail, we managed to drag together enough semi-musicians to play the New Year's Eve gig at the Wheelhouse, climaxing in the Hully-Gully and the unveiling of a gorgeous girl in a bikini. (I had somehow driven this girl, between sets, up to her home in Parkstone where she stripped off and put on her Happy New Year outfit, then back to The Wheelhouse, all without me touching her ... how did she do that? And what was her name? Lesley.)

But it couldn't last. If we were going anywhere by way of making music, be it for fun or profit, we needed to be in a proper group: one with proper musicians, some degree of musical focus, and at least a modicum of management – not to mention a drummer. I was in no position to provide any of these things. I was in chaotic shock – the mix of post-Leeds intellectual vacuum, music overload, casual emotionally charged sex, booze, bus conducting ... I was in no state for anything except to stumble down whatever enticing, thrillingly dangerous alley happened to open up before me.

One of Bob's talents was to search out and inveigle his way into obscure, sleazy night time venues hidden away in the back-street alleyways of Bournemouth and Boscombe. There was a red-lit upstairs room, with tuxedoed waiters and a smarmy host, where we would sit for hours nursing an over-priced lager and listening to some plonky cocktail piano trio, because Bob thought we had a contact. There was a confusion here, in which I probably connived – if you had a 'contact', in other words speaking terms with someone less than six degrees away from someone in the music business, then you were on your way to success. The product would come afterwards. This idea would come back to haunt me, not to mention the entire music industry, later.

One of these 'clubs' was in the basement of the Burlington, a huge pre-war red brick hotel in Boscombe, recently converted into apartments. I don't think I went there more than three times. As a place to spend an exciting evening, it rated low. In fact, as a place to spend any kind of evening it rated low. But the third time, a trivial event changed my life.

A group was rehearsing, and we were allowed in to listen. They started on a passable version of *All My Loving*, except that the guitarist clearly wasn't up to Lennon's rhythm triplets, and they didn't have a lead to do the solo. I recognised this lack of competence immediately, even though I'd only heard the song maybe twice. Then they moved on to another number. This was, unbelievably, Cliff Richard's *Move It*. I'd spent hours mastering this, back in 1958. I watched them floundering around for a while, and finally had to jump up in frustration. "I can show you how to do that intro if you want", I said to the guitarist. He grinned. "Go on then." So I borrowed his guitar, and showed him.

It became a short jam session, I think one or two Chuck Berry numbers. I hadn't played much with anyone but Bob for ages, and there was a real release in having, for the first time ever, a proper drummer behind me. I linked in with Lee immediately. I remember to this day our first eye contact, that rhythmic click that told me that making music was, above all, a form of communication.

Afterwards, Lee's dad Eric 'Pops' Kerslake bought us a beer. It became apparent that this had been an audition, dropped in from the capricious waves of fortune. Several sets of needs had fortuitously crash-landed together in this unlikely seedy venue. Pops wanted a group for his drummer boy, and was out for the best he could find; Bob and I wanted a group, any group. In the first of my several succumbments to persuasive managers, a deal was somehow wrangled out there and then. It would be a six-piece pop group, consisting of Tony (vocals), Lee (drums), Bill (bass), Graham (rhythm guitar – for some forgotten reason we called him Sid), Bob (piano) and me (lead guitar). Pops would arrange for any equipment – amps, instruments, transport – to be supplied, and would of course act as booking agent. All we had to do was come up with the music.

Well, all that came to pass, in a rush. Suddenly I had a nice Vox AC30 amp, and Bob had a Hohner electric piano (which made a lovely if not entirely appropriate sound), and we were gathered together in a Temperance Hall in Boscombe to get a repertoire together. I went through a couple of new guitars and ended up with my blond Telecaster, bought on hire purchase from Eddie Moors in Boscombe, not Don Strike from whom I'd got all my guitars until then. Perversely, the main reason I wanted a Tele was through my admiration for Andy Summers, then playing slick jazz solos on his in Zoot Money's Big Roll Band at the Disque-aGoGo late-nighters, using the soft pick-up setting (the antithesis of the Telecaster's true role as a country-slicker or power rhythm instrument). If I'd chosen a Strat or a Gibson or a Rickenbacker my life might have been altogether different.

The group was christened, inadvertently, by me. One day (I think it was the day I got the Tele) I walked in to Lee's parents' house with mud on my shoes. "Ooh, look at Tim's track marks on my carpet", said his mum. The rest is history. We were the Trackmarks.

PRESENTING THE

TRACKMARKS

The repertoire turned out to be an intriguing mishmash. The core consisted of timely, finely analysed and meticulously performed covers of whatever chart hits we deemed appropriate. We did Beatles, Searchers, Animals, Kinks, better than they did. The group's seemingly bloated line-up actually added to our reproductive capabilities, because my analytical skills came into play – I was the musical director. I could listen to a record and somehow extract the key sonic elements, the key lines which a six-piece band could deploy to recreate the feel of the original 45 whilst making it sound louder, riskier, better.

For example, if you listen to *You Really Got Me* on 45, it actually sounds quite thin, and the famous solo is tinny and a bit distant (studio engineers were terrified of going into red). I boosted the riff by getting Sid to thrash it on his Rickenbacker (only a six-string – if it had been a twelve I'd now gladly track him down and offer him half the universe for it) down at the nut end, Bob to use the lowest register of the Hohner in single note piano bass, whilst I doubled it at the top end of the Tele, gently, waiting to cut loose on the best impersonation I could manage of (legend has it) Jimmy Page's storming minimalist solo. Billy, meanwhile, was frustratedly waiting for his chance to be Paul McCartney, or Charles Mingus.

The one area we were weak in was vocals. Tony was a competent lead singer, but backing harmonies, which were, are and always will be a staple of pop music, were carried more or less single-voicedly by me – half-heartedly, because I didn't think I could sing. Sid may have tried a bit. The idea of singing was anathema to the others. So the Trackmarks were never going to be the next Searchers.

Apart from this pop-based core, and much more significantly, we were exploring the same back territory as every other group of the time. We went to the Bure Club at Highcliffe (where I tripped over a gate-stop and fell on my right hand onto gravel, earning a little scar I still sport today, a relic and a trophy and a caution) to hear John Lee Hooker on one of his many U.K. tours with the Groundhogs. ('Can't even complete a twelve-bar' was an overheard comment, spectacularly missing the whole point of Hooker's unique redefinition of the blues.) There was a local group called the Soul Brothers who specialised in dynamics: they'd take a tune like *Spoonful* way down until you could hardly hear them, then build the volume up a bit, then slam you with a blast of ear-damaging trebly noise led by crash cymbals and high scrubbed guitar – then take it back down again ... I tried to get the Trackmarks to do this. (Cream did something like it four years later.) The blues intrigued and seduced me. *Smokestack Lightning* struck me like nothing much had since *Heartbreak Hotel*.

Pops started to get us some gigs. We were very big in Swanage, the Drill Hall. I went through great loves and numerous Swanage girls. I was still living at home, still conducting buses as my day and night job. A bus conductor had to work prescribed shifts, which you could only get out of by swapping commitments with other bus conductors, via an arcane underground network of contacts and secret negotiations. I guess that most bus conductors were adept at this – but they didn't have to map an unpredictable Trackmarks gig schedule onto it. I suppose I must have been a key element of the group, because my enforced absences became a problem. Rather than sack me, Pops solved this problem by fixing me up with an office-boy job at a glass works in Winton (being over-qualified, I had to tell embarrassing lies to secure this).

So, I settled in to the nine to five, rehearsals at weekends, gigs whenever they came along and were achievable. The Morris Minor with the red leather had more or less become mine – I would ask my mother if she needed it, the usual answer being no, but don't come home too late, and put petrol in. We still went down the Wheelhouse, El Cabala, and increasingly a heaving downstairs pub called the Badger, off the Old Christchurch Road. The bowling alley was also a good late night hangout, where visiting girls from London and beyond could be found. Weekends, if there wasn't a gig, we would drive out to remote Dorset pubs like the Worlds

End, where we'd get pissed on scrumpy and then drive back home.

'Settled in'. It seems strange now to think back to the details of that wild time and see that it was, in fact, mostly staid and boring. My intellectual pretensions from Leeds had all but evaporated in the warmth of imaginary pop stardom; I didn't think much at all. Actually, the day job was quite interesting – I analysed and improved the supply chain system of the glass shop, whilst learning a lot about glass. I flirted with the plump little office girl, and stole small amounts of petty cash when I thought I could get away with it. But I was settled in. The job was steady; the group was steady, keeping up with the covers and the Howling Wolf regurgitations: I'd fallen back into a pattern.

Behind all that, my life was precarious. My mother still hadn't accepted or enabled my freedom: that I could live at home, paying rent, but allowed to behave like an independent adult. (She was probably right.) The first time I stayed out all night, I had to phone in early next morning with made-up excuses. My father was so angry we didn't speak for weeks. I moved out for a couple of days to a rented room off the Holdenhurst Road, then quickly ducked back home, persuaded by my brother, once I'd sobered up and realised just how appallingly awful that life would have been. I hitched up to Leeds and back, twice, which didn't help either. On the gigs, I was going through the motions. Chuck Berry solos and Jimmy Reed boogie riffs are actually quite easy to play once you've established the templates. As I've said, analysing pieces and tutoring the musicians to perform their parts is also easy for me. I worked out *Everything's All*

Right by the Mojos, and *Right String Baby But The Wrong Yoyo* by the Moquettes, in all their intricate detail, and forced the Trackmarks to emulate these well-crafted records in every detail of my enhanced analysis.

In a parallel lane, another kind of music was racing up, headlights blazing, fuelled on jazz and blues and not giving a toss about pop. We called it r&b, rhythm and blues – the bastard child of all those disturbing, electrifying records I'd been hearing two years before, the weird jazz, the raw blues, the smooth Mose Allison grooves.

The Disque a Go!Go! was a damp smelly cellar at 9 Holdenhurst Road, just up from the Lansdowne, accessed down a steep firetrap staircase. It had been opened as a jazz venue, the Downstairs Club, in 1961, but by the time we started to frequent it, it was all about this r&b stuff. The club was run by an enthusiastic entrepreneurial Italian amateur impresario called Tony Silvestro. The Disque was configured, I think, on the model of the Cavern in Liverpool – low ceiling, soapbox stage, minimalist refreshments up back supplied by Tracey, sweating walls, illegal electrics and fire hazards, tons of sweaty entranced kids – but hundreds of miles away musically. At the Disque, r&b ruled. Zoot Money, The Nite People, Geno Washington, Tony Colton, Herbie Goins, Ronnie Jones and the Night-Timers – they all played the Saturday late-nighters. So too, once, did the Trackmarks.

We were support to Zoot. It was a disaster. We were drunk and nervous, and the heat and humidity put my guitar irretrievably out of tune. We'd never played a small room like this, and the balance was shot to hell. The repertoire was also unfocussed; this crowd, high on cool jazzy Hammond organ based stuff as delivered by the Big Roll Band, weren't there to hear slick covers of the Kinks. After the set, Andy Summers commiserated with me about the guitar tuning nightmare, but that only made it worse.

The lead-in to my exit from the Trackmarks was a low point in my musical career. I was hubristic, believing myself to be a star (I was getting the sex, wasn't I?), while not actually putting in the graft and the hours. My playing suffered from lack of practice and from too much booze. The other Trackmarks, I was convinced, were conspiring behind my back. Pops paid me back-handed compliments about my playing skills, which I stupidly took at face value. Bob, I felt, was up to something – he spent much more time with Bill than with me, what was that about? I was excluded from rehearsals. I remember once turning up accidentally, to meet Greg Lake guiltily exiting from a Trackmarks session. (He sat down with me and showed me how to do a diminished arpeggio run on the guitar. I suspect the history of the music universe would have been slightly different if he'd got the job – think of a world without ELP ...)

Meanwhile my musical inclinations were spinning all over the place. With Bob, I was getting more and more into modern jazz, whilst understanding it less and less. Motown and Stax soul were creeping in – Dick and I bought two US import compilations, one on Tamla, the other on Motown, of early Detroit hits (I still have them), and Otis Redding and Joe Tex and Wilson Pickett had begun to surface. The Disque all-nighter bands were doing even more obscure stuff by people like Junior Lance and Ike and Tina Turner. And one incredible night The Who played the Disque.

The dent in the wall, when Townshend drove the neck end of his guitar into it with wilful deliberate destructiveness, is still there in my memory (though not in the long-demolished club). The fat Italian DJ, used to putting on cool jazz LPs by people like Art Blakey, pronounced the death of music. I was enthralled. How could anybody dare to do that? To have that brazen contempt for the tools and techniques of their trade? And how could those jazzers, Coltrane, Davis, play those ineluctable cascades? And those sweet thumping sounds from Detroit and Memphis, and those spinning, accelerating lyrics? The times were indeed changing, at a vertiginous rate.

But my own times were ready to shift into an entirely different gear.

The Making of the Moods

The Trackmarks, at least as far as I was concerned, were done for. Musical directions were spinning off all over the place, in the whole universe as well as the band, whilst mutterings began and continued. I knew something was happening, but I didn't know what it was. When Bob and Bill called me to a meeting to inform me that, after due consideration, they'd decided after all to appoint me to be the guitar player in this new band they'd decided to form, which would be doing this new organ and brass-led stuff like Zoot, like the Nite People, I just assumed this was the natural course. I hardly noticed the edge I'd been teetering on – becoming deputy manager of a glass shop, after maybe five or six years' apprenticeship.

The parting from the Trackmarks was gentle, unacrimonious. Eric Kerslake rightly reclaimed my Vox amp, so I had to go to Don Strike to get a replacement, a Fender Tremolux. I'd being paying, somehow, for the Tele myself. Bob managed to retain his Hohner Pianette. At the time, I had no idea what became of the group, didn't even think about it. (Websites suggest that they reformed and carried on for a while, and Lee of course went on to the glories of Uriah Heep.) I'm very good at forgetting and moving on, as long as there's something in my mind's eye to move on towards.

So Bob, Billy and me became a team. Well, there wasn't anyone else! I'd have recruited Lee as the drummer, but obviously that wasn't on. (I've seen suggestions on the internet that Lee played with DAM, but this never happened. Unfortunately.) So we needed a drummer, and a brass section. One day, Bob remembered a school friend of his called Andy Kirk.

Andy was the younger son in a well-to-do family in Wareham, his father being the local country solicitor. As younger sons will be, Andy, although having had a fine education at Canford (the public school my parents had groomed me for but failed to get me admitted to, thank the Lord, back in 1953), was the classic black sheep scion of the Kirk clan. He was dragged round to Bob's for a chat. Andy played trumpet, or cornet (I still don't quite know the difference). He was unemployed. With his friend Graham Livermore, he gigged with local trad jazz bands, in which he usually held up the lead trumpet role and occasionally rose to inspired solos.

Graham, trombone, was a steady reliable musician. I stress that word, musician. He was seriously into those notes which sat behind the chords, and striving against his limited technique to find them, and play them. (Years later, we'd have this conversation: Me: "You know, even Coltrane and Rollins and such, you can hear them repeating themselves. Re-using the same phrases." Graham: "Yeah. I know. (pause) Wish I knew what they were.") He came from a poor background, and was holding down a stultifying day job to do, I think, with canned food. He'd recently got married, not perhaps in ideal circumstances, but music was his first, perhaps only, love.

So this wasn't the ideal brass section – compare the Blue Flames or the Big Roll Band, consummate technicians who would collaborate in rehearsal and then construct, write and read a chart. The norm was trumpet, tenor sax, baritone sax – we had a trombonist (bizarre at the time, which goes to show how easily stereotypes get constructed and set in hardening mud, if not stone) instead of the baritone. But we had two-thirds of a brass section, five-eights of a band.

We were looking for a drummer, and a sax player, and a singer. I think the drummer must have come first – John, another of Bob's finds. I just remember turning up to one of the Sunday morning practice sessions at Bob's mother's house in Montague Road to find this shy, taciturn guy setting up his huge Ludwig kit in the front room, confident and ready to drum. We soon found that he was way ahead of any other drummers we'd considered – technique following Buddy Rich, his drum hero, and a big fat sound. He was a shoo-in. I think I had some vague doubts: he didn't improvise enough for my taste, content just to hold the beat and follow the chart; other drummers would listen more to the rest of the band, especially when a bit of a jam got going. (Not that we were doing any of that yet – we were still working on just playing together and establishing a very basic repertoire, raw materials. My Monk'n'Django impro days with Bob were gone forever.) It took years to uncover John's downside.

We tried out a couple of sax players. Then Pete Sweet turned up from nowhere, probably again through Andy and Graham's jazz networks. Pete was an unlikely candidate for the job. For a start, he was old, in his early forties. Secondly, he was settled, married, owned a guesthouse in Southbourne Road, Stella Maris. But we all took to each other at once. Now, I'd be tempted to suggest that he was in a Harley Davison mid-life crisis, if he hadn't come across as so laid back. Pete was tubby, balding, played tenor, and understood this jazz stuff, those changes, in a way that none of the rest of us ever got anywhere near to. Later, he'd explain to me how the song *Inchworm*, from the Danny Kaye film about Hans Christian Andersen, moved chromatically down through the scale for a few notes, then jumped back up; and how you could put those underlying chords (diminished minors, augmented majors) to use, to create a totally new melody line. I understood, gleefully absorbed Pete's musical insights. I could do it in my head, still can, but I never have managed to ship that from my musical brain to my guitar fingers. Except late in the evening, on my own, when I occasionally imagine that it's happening.

Pete was happy to join the band, for evening gigging purposes. God knows what arrangements he made with his wife about running Stella Maris. If we started off as a confused 'Beatles meet the Nite People via the Trackmarks', he surely added some necessary grown-up focus to our post-teenage confusion. I have no real idea where the other guys were, musically, but I have a very clear picture of where I was, which was all over the place. How can you be in a band like this whilst digging The Who? But Pete Sweet's obvious love and enthusiasm for the kind of stuff we all had in the back of our minds must have carried us over, because next thing I knew, we were becoming a tight outfit, firmly based in the territory Georgie, Zoot and the others had staked out, but starting to pull in material from other, as yet unexplored, directions.

We didn't really have a name. 'The Trane Set' is one I recall, which neatly sums up our fuzzy focus. I mischievously suggested we abbreviate this to 'The Tea Set'. I was still the singer. We rehearsed a few numbers (James Brown stuff, Georgie Fame copies – I did creditable covers of his versions of *Eso Beso* and *Moody's Mood for Love*) – and actually managed, through Bob's machinations, to get a gig or two. I was, of course, still working at the glassworks, and did one gig with the tip of my middle finger, left hand, plastered from a glass-handling accident; try that whilst singing and playing guitar.

• • •

Dave Anthony was a local legend as a singer, alongside Tony Blackburn (one of my late fifties pick-up groups backed Blackburn for a Drill Hall gig, to no avail – you'll never know the break you missed there, Tone). Dave had fronted local groups from way back. Tony and the Ramrods, Dave Anthony and the Ravers. He was briefly in an obscure band called The

Dave Anthony's Moods

Sands Combo, along with George 'Zoot' Money, and another called The League of Gentlemen, in which early incarnation he may or may not have overlapped with Bob (later Robert) Fripp – the history is murky.

Whatever, in those early days, while most of us were still scratching around for a drummer, a gig, some A levels or degrees, Dave Anthony was out there with real groups, playing real rock'n'roll. He had a rasping soul baritone voice, reminiscent of Ray Charles or Solomon Burke; he was awesome. So when Bob discovered, through his mysterious, arcane networks, that Dave had broken up his current band and was searching for musical direction, Bob pounced.

Somehow, Dave was contacted, wooed, and eventually persuaded to come round to Montague Road for a chat. I wasn't there at this meeting, but it transpired that Dave had a concept in mind, suggested by a building site mate of his called Graham: a repertoire which would somehow reflect the many facets of his personality, feelings and circumstances, through a set of songs which would be performed live, cabaret-style, and eventually become the first ever concept album... Good job I wasn't there, really.

Dave's concept would, he explained, be called 'Dave Anthony's Moods'.

Local

Photo by Al Kirtley

THE DOWNSTAIRS CLUB
LATER LE DISQUE A GO! GO!

BOURNEMOUTH'S FIRST FULL-TIME
ROCK AND JAZZ VENUE OPENED
3 MAY 1961 IN THE BASEMENT OF
9 HOLDENHURST ROAD

MANFRED MANN, ERIC CLAPTON,
THE WHO, GEORGIE FAME,
ZOOT MONEY, ANDY SUMMERS
AND MANY OTHER MUSICIANS
PLAYED HERE

UNVEILED 2014

Bournemouth was still Bournemouth, Southbourne still Southbourne. The cliffs, the beach, Old Harry, the Polar Bear hadn't moved or changed, nor had most of the shops and pavements. The sea had both moved and changed, but still looked and felt the same. The girls came and went and sometimes came back. As spring 1965 moved towards summer, I fell back into my old pattern of indolence, inertia, going with the flow, something I do well. Up at eight to be at the office by nine (in the old Morris Minor, which had more or less become my car by default); hard day at the glass-face (I got through the entire works of Harold Robbins at my desk); sometimes in the evening up to Bob's for rehearsals, other times out with the current girl. I don't think I ever spent an evening at home, that would've felt quite strange. I don't think I deliberately saw a single television programme from 1958 (Quatermass) until 1970 when I came back from Italy. La Fiesta was long dead. El Cabala in Old Christchurch Road was the coffee bar, they had a juke-box nearly as well stashed as the Wheelhouse (which was still just about going – *Wipeout* by the Surfaris hit the box, almost as big an influence as Link Wray's *Rumble* eight years before). I got in with a guy called Alan, a wide boy who was well into the Beach Boys, another musical influence I'd completely missed till I heard tracks like *The Warmth of the Sun*, which took me all the way back to vaguely remembered stuff like the Four Freshmen, the kind of music my sister had moved on to in the mid-fifties when I was busy discovering Elvis, and opened up yet another spectrum of harmonies, in which you could somehow impose six nearly adjacent notes and create, not a discord, but a magical new sonic screen which, crucially, contained the additional, third element of popular music, the words. *The Warmth of the Sun*, as an orchestral piece, would have been a lovely snippet of Tchaikovsky, great changes and top melody line – as a pop song with its lyrics ('the love of my life has left me today... still I have the warmth of the sun'), it's a concentrated, distilled emotion. Alan and I cruised and picked up the occasional holiday surfer girl from Wales or West Bromwich.

The other main place we hung out was The Badger, which I've already mentioned. It was a huge downstairs cellar pub, made of clean spit and sawdust and rough wood bars and tables, long counter serving cheap beer by the yard, off the Old Christchurch Road just below Horseshoe Common, where all the Bournemouth youth would gravitate about eight every Friday and Saturday night to pick up grapevine hints about where there might be some kind of party, usually up in the

Canford Cliffs, where the rich girls lived. The beer was cheap, and at 7.45 the place was packed enough to make it difficult to fall over, if you needed to. By 8.30, it was empty, except for the saddos who'd missed the hints. I probably broke even on that front, but there was sometimes a tug of conflict – I'd picked up a hint, but Bob and Bill and whoever else I was with hadn't; and I had the wheels, but not enough room for everyone, and anyway I wanted to keep the back seat empty, just in case of a rich girl. (Happened twice to be exact. Don't ask for names.)

. . .

We managed to shoot down Dave's pretensions and get him to become part of the band, component rather than leader. We started to know him by his real name, Tony. Of course he didn't really accept this inside himself, any more than Bob or I had. So we had three leaders, none of them declared. For the time being this didn't matter much – we were fired up with the music, with the unparalleled thrill of finding a song no-one else had done, working up our own take on the arrangement, rehearsing it until it was tight as a snare skin, and finally taking it out to some smoky, seedy locale for it to be unleashed on an unprepared audience.

From the start, what we aimed for was power. No tinkly pussy-footed jazzy jams for us – we wanted to be loud heavyweight punchers. John's musical genesis was big-band swing, those percussive horn parts, sledgehammer dynamics and calculated drum fills – he brought this to the band by simply doing it, no talk, lead from the back. So perhaps we had four leaders: perhaps we had eight. In those early days, it didn't matter. Eight guys, each with his own internal agenda and pulling towards his own direction – for a while, a fairly long while, these eight contrary forces added up, like some nutty seventeenth century physics experiment, to a single pull in a single direction.

Those rehearsal sessions at Bob's were intense. We forged musical tracks into our heads, rapidly. When you listen to that stuff on record now, it sounds simple. But back then it was necessary to analyse and recreate the complexity behind. Listen to *I Feel Good, Loving You Too Long, My Girl,* Duffy Power's version of Jimmy Reed's *Bright Lights, Big City* (I can't trace this fabulous record anywhere, though I know it existed; memories outlast the merely physical) – the artistry behind a great record isn't that easy to recapture. Especially as we had to add that extra element of big-band power. I knew somehow that this component was going to distinguish us from the rest, and I was right. James Brown sounded somehow a bit weak on record. Live, our reproduction of *I Feel Good* seemed to possess the force to have blown Bob's mother's front room into the stratosphere. But this still had to be tested, live, against the public.

The breakthrough came when, after a few try-out gigs, we secured the regular Saturday late-nighter at the Disque a Go!Go! However it came about – The Nite People, previous incumbents, having moved on or broken up – in a very quick intense burst of negotiation, where all the components were spun around like swirling 78 grooves, ending up in the middle of the Disque, somehow Dave Anthony's Moods got the gig, the Saturday late session.

There's nothing like a good regular spot like that to forge a band's tightness and intuition into a finely honed piece of well-engineered machinery, powered by telepathy. Hard work though. We'd turn up at eight o'clock, hump the kit down the very narrow stairs into the firetrap and set up on the narrow platform stage, repair to the Lansdowne pub across the road for a few pints, then return at ten to play our expanding repertoire through to the early hours. The party pick-ups at the Badger went by the board, but that was OK – the rich girls were coming to us. Actually, me and Andy were probably the only ones of the eight to be actively predatory. Graham and Pete were married. Tony was married, but led his own off-duty life. Bill and John were mysteries, went home after work. Bob was just Bob.

I know we had other local gigs, but try as I may I can't remember a single one. Maybe we played the Bure Club, once. The Disque late-nighter was all it took to get us fired up. Every single week the place was heaving with action, of every kind I'm sure, though at this stage I was blissfully ignorant and innocent of any drugs stronger than beer and sex. Scary-eyed girls full of pills circled around me, but when Jeff Cooper eventually paired me up to one of them, Maria, I soon found that she was a nice Catholic daughter who didn't really like booze that much, never mind barbiturates (she liked the sex though). Maria may have been my introduction to the disappointment that goes with inflated expectation – you're told this is going to be wild, dangerous, then when it actually happens you think 'is that it'? I think I went with her largely through this temptation towards perilous unexplored realms, and she let me down. The last time I saw her (before she sacked me by letter) she was going to knit me a sweater.

Reading back, I see I haven't gone into details about most of my girls. Well, this isn't supposed to be that kind of memoir, and isn't going to turn into one. But it would be dishonest to exclude them – the spirit of rock'n'roll, after all, springs from sex: look it up. I won't deliberately introduce them merely to illustrate my narrative, to prove my super-stud status, to prove that this was the Sixties. They'll turn up when they want to, like Maria just did.

• • •

Somewhere in the spring of 65 we decided that we were ready to go professional. In the maelstrom of my personal life, this was momentous. It meant I had to quit the glass day job, cut loose from my support structures (home, car, food), take off into the risk of the unknown. Leeds had been merely a rehearsal for what was to come – the back-packing round-the-world fantasy was exposed, this was for real. It meant cutting out into self sufficiency or into failure and oblivion. It meant moving to London.

London and Beyond

M y getaway was a bit complicated. As is my way, I introverted, focussing on my own problems. A checklist of those problems during those intense weeks could read something like 'resign from glassworks job; help order and organise stage outfits; tell parents; sort out complicated girlfriend situations; everything else'.

As is also my way, I let this list fester in my mind for several weeks, until it all came together in the space of about three days. The stage kits, striped blazers in Bournemouth School brown-and-blue, were ordered from a cheap clothes shop in Old Christchurch Road. They had to be collected at a particular time on a particular Tuesday, so I faked a puncture and turned up very late to work. Mr Smith called me into his inner sanctum office. I got my words in first: "Sorry not to give you more notice, but I'm leaving next week". He smiled, a bit thinly. "Just as well, I was thinking about it too. You can't do two jobs at the same time."

I rapidly covered the traces of my petty larceny, organised a leaving celebration – I'm sure I brought several bottles into the shop, to the delight of the office girls and the frowns of Mr Watkins, the decrepit office manager I'd been supposed to be understudying – walked out and drove home, without an ounce of regret. Looking back though, I reckon Mr Smith contained an ounce or two of envy.

'Tell parents' was of course the hard one. We were communicating, if at all, via a third party (my brother). There's a streak of cowardice in my make-up, or perhaps over-indulgence in strategy – either way, I do put things off, scary things, until it's almost too late, or beyond. So it was that I told them, just in time, that I'd quit the glass job and was off to London, next week, to seek my fortune.

They went ape. Their fortune, the one they'd spent on the captain of industry, was going to be squandered on a bottomless pit of worthless trashy whimsical fantasy. Of course, they didn't put it that eloquently. My father actually chased me round the table with a virtual machete, spouting the only real swearwords (Fs and Bs, I don't think any Cs) I ever heard him use, before or since. Eventually we calmed down. One of my mother's perennial expressions about me was 'once he's dug his heels in…': I dug them in quite deeply. Most of the other parents, not having the same expectation set, were actually quite supportive, and of course I played on that. Eventually, they came around. She was torn, about me, between that captain and her father: the intellectual and the artistic sides of what she saw as my genetic inheritance. 'What's bred in the bone' could have been my mother's lifetime leitmotif. If it wasn't inherited, she denied it. I'm making her sound simplistic, I know; that's because I only really remember her in extremis, plotting her children's own voyages on their behalf when she believed the tide was high. She should have gone into politics. That would have focussed her intelligence beyond her family. Oh well.

• • •

We obviously needed to live somewhere. So we got hold of the Evening Standard, which had a 'property to let' section in its classifieds. We picked one out, and Bob phoned up Mr Adlard, the landlord of 17 Hutchings Walk, Hampstead Garden Suburb, and explained that we're an eight piece r&b band who're going pro, going to be huge, and so need to live in London – we're in management negotiations, expect to break into the big time, and meanwhile we're confident, really, we can honestly demonstrate enough on the income stream to pay at least the first few months, some of it in advance, so can we rent your house please, Mr Adlard?

We had no income, no management, no demonstrable prospects of any kind. Mad. Bob and I attended an interview with him at a hotel somewhere in the West End, on a day trip. Mr Adlard was in his forties, something in the City, lived out in Radlett, Herts, but still owned this four bedroom detached house in, actually, a bit more East Finchley than Hampstead Garden Suburb. He looked and talked like a WW2 fighter pilot. He asked searching questions, got intelligently made-up answers, was clearly highly amused by the whole caper. He must have recognised some kind of quality, or else was as mad or stupid as us, who knows. Anyway, that day we somehow secured and signed a six month lease, starting next week. We hadn't even seen the house.

I'll never know how Pete and Graham convinced their wives that they had to walk away and come to London. Musical fire is the only viable explanation, especially for Pete. Graham was married because he had a child, and so had a kind of excuse, whereas Pete was married long-term, running a business (there were kids, but they'd have been irrelevant in my thinking at the time, he was an incongruous old man who was also a friend who happened to play astonishing tenor). The others were more or less free to go, though Billy, I think, had a bit of trouble cutting the apron strings. And Tony had his own agenda, which he didn't share, yet.

Whilst we were negotiating our accommodation, we were also negotiating our business. At that time, usual practice was that you needed a manager, and you needed an agency. The former guided your career and, if you were lucky, financed initial capital outlays such as, in our case, a van, Bob's ancient Bedford being on its last legs and certainly not up to long-haul; the latter got you the gigs. Sometimes the two roles were performed by the same people, in other cases there was usually a close tie-in between two separate outfits. But in the mid-sixties 'the band-beat business', as Andy's brother Tim once charmingly denoted it, was shuddering from the Beatles' seismic revolution. New business models were emerging, evolving or dissolving back into the miasma they'd sprung from, with bewildering effervescence. Of course, we knew very little of this. We just knew we needed a manager, and some gigs.

Scouts were out across the universe, tracking down the next big one. We must have got spotted (I vaguely recall a couple of mysterious men in suits lurking at the back of the Disque one Saturday), because next thing we knew we were being courted by no less than four big or emerging names, of fascinatingly different flavours.

The Gunnell brothers were said to own the West End club scene, to have it sewn up, Kray-style gangster model. They had most of those bands who'd been our inspirations, like Georgie Fame or Zoot Money, on tightly reined contracts. The Flamingo in Wardour Street was their showcase and nerve centre, from which their web, propelled by rumour and fear, spread across the land (or at least as far as Brixton). At the interview, once we'd played coy, Ric smiled, said "you know you'll end up with us eventually, don't you?", while Johnny stood at the door and fingered his cheek scar. We smiled and trembled out of the office. This prediction would turn out to be weirdly, perversely accurate.

Robert Stigwood was Australian. His business model, therefore, was a precursor of Murdoch's. Build a concept around an image and market it – the product can come later, and be manipulated at will. He and his 'people' didn't seem to have much of a clue about music, especially ours. After the mid-morning interview in a posh Mayfair office, champagne was issued all round, for all the world as if some contract had just been signed. We were impressed by the champagne.

The wild card was Tony Seconda. In an intimate, smoky session in his West End flat, he and I had a great conversation

Dave Anthony's Moods

about the stuff that was emerging from California – Byrds, Jefferson Airplane, Lovin' Spoonful and such – whilst the others nodded and smiled. With hindsight, I should have cut and run there and then: 'yes please, I want that.' But then Seconda blew it by replying, to some chance question, "we could be looking at the next Tom Jones here". Well, if Dave Anthony's eyes might just have lit up, everyone else's dimmed.

And then there was Ken Pitt. Old style manager, suit and tie, no champagne, no dangerous associates, office in Shepherd's Market (a high class red light area at the time), exuded cultured homosexual charm. His main claim to fame, apart from being part of the tin pan alley establishment rather than one of these upstart new boys, was that he managed Manfred Mann, who were hugely successful at the time, achieving the crossover from rhythm and blues to eventual pop stardom of a sort. (Most of us hated them for this: how could anyone move as far from their principles as they did with that *Doo Wah Diddy* crap, and still claim authenticity? Bob, though, was in love with Manfred, organ freaks both, who needed three quarters of the van for their B3s and Leslies. Unknown to us, at this time they were also conspiring to sack Pitt – which would transpire to be the story of his career, as David Bowie can tell you. But that's another tale, which has been told.)

Pitt was realistic about our prospects. We were in a crowded market niche, competing against many similar, far more established acts, and he wasn't issuing guarantees. But his tie-in booking agency, London City, had a steadily loyal venue list, could offer us some reliable repeat gigs, had good relations with the Gunnells (who'd made it clear there'd be no hard feelings) and with Georgio Gomelsky, so we could get into the Flamingo, the Ram Jam, the Marquee, the 100 Club... As importantly, he was willing to take a bit of a risk, would buy us a new van, and sub us for the Hutchings Walk rent, at least for a while.

Pitt prevailed. My ego, stupidly seduced by the promise of instant stardom, wanted to go with Stigwood. My head, on the rare occasions it was working, said go with the Gunnells, because they can guarantee money. My musical heart, that tiny concentrated leftover from those early musical formations, I think was telling me that Tony Seconda was offering a quite different direction, new dangerous stuff which didn't exist yet; I would've had to have been braver than I was to go that route. So common sense prevailed. We signed up with Ken Pitt. Actually, there wasn't a real choice – Bob had already made it.

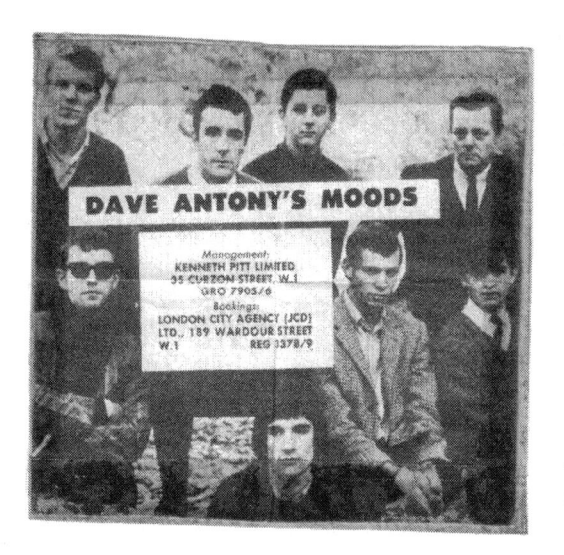

Records, my squiggly first loves, were quite forgotten for now.

•••

There was a gig in transit from Bournemouth to London, in some kind of shed in Reading – I think we played a blinder, blinded by the prospects of this freedom we were storming into. We then got to our new home, probably dropped onto the floor whatever kit we'd brought in the back of the old van, probably dropped ourselves on top of it and, possibly, slept. In fact, I remember that: drunk, exhilarated, falling onto the floor on top of some kind of sleeping bag package…

The next night, we played our inaugural gig at the Flamingo. The Flamingo! I have no idea how this booking was arranged; it certainly can't have been by Pitt or London City, so perhaps it was one of those murky Disque suits, or perhaps Bob just phoned Ric Gunnell…

We were support to who knows who. We were allowed into the so-called dressing room, a cupboard stage left, packed solid with musicians just come off or waiting to go on. When I went out to get a Coke I was punched in the face (not very hard) by a huge black guy who felt I'd hassled him, jumped a queue, something. I said "sorry!" – why? he'd assaulted me – he said something like "be careful 'round here," a warning I possibly over-heeded for a while. When I got back to the dressing room with my Coke, there was a rather funny smell in there.

17 Hutchings Walk turned out to be a very respectable inner-suburb dwelling – detached, on a corner, tucked away behind a nice little strip of shops (baker, butcher, paper shop), just a short drive away from the A1 and handy for the Northern Line. A house with four bedrooms was adapted to sleep eight, with importation of extra beds and intricately negotiated partnerships. I was on an excruciatingly uncomfortable camp

bed, sharing with John and Bill (the room, not the bed), for several months. Tony, without consultation or negotiation, imported his Italian wife Anna and their baby David, so they had to have a room to themselves. I suppose Andy, Graham and Pete must have bunked together in bedroom four. Bob installed some kind of folding bed in the back end of the sitting/dining room, on his own.

Once we settled into this weird kind of domesticity, gigs not being that frequent in these early days, eating communally (corned beef hash, industrial sized catering packs of cornflakes from Pete's Cash and Carry in Boscombe, occasional forays down the parade of shops in Falloden Way for the guilty pleasure of a solitary steak and salad), finding our way to the lovely, dusty, faded plush pub at East Finchley tube and downing two or three pints on borrowed funds and time (I went back there in 1970, during a job-seeking London visit; it was exactly the same; I wouldn't dare to try that today) – I started to grow into this new family. I suppose we made friends with each other, mostly. There were tiffs and fights. We had a small telly, owned by Tony and Anna. Much later, the 1966 World Cup Final obviously had to be watched, but because of some kind of infringement of some arcane rule nobody else knew about, five minutes before kick-off she confiscated the TV. Or tried to. I think this was one Italian matriarchal move too far. We watched the match. England won 4 – 2.

We all smoked as much tobacco as we could manage. Five Woodbines from the newsagent's down the parade would be stretched out to seven by recycling of dog-ends into Rizlas. I was, and am, an addict, to tobacco and to alcohol. Strangely, it's not the physical substances that enslave me – I go for weeks and months without a fag (rather less without a drink, I have to admit, but it has been done without noticeable withdrawal symptoms) – but the process of indulging, the ritual of opening the fag packet, American style soft packs being preferred, squashed in a back pocket, extracting the carefully selected stick, straightening it out and giving it that little tap just like James Bond or the Saint, then firing up the Zippo or the cerini… after all that, the actual smoking of the cigarette is an incidental. And of course drugs hadn't even appeared on the horizon yet. That making and unmaking of the band was way up ahead.

Work, as we called it, came in slowly. London City had a solid though limited venue base, built upon the old style music business model, and also, because they were nice guys, good links with other agencies who were more than happy to swap vacant slots. But if there was any kind of contention, DAM up against Graham Bond or someone at the Marquee for instance, it's clear who was going to get first shot. We did actually play support at the Marquee a few times, once to The Move, Tony Seconda's new project, whose gimmick was to smash up a television set live on stage – cheaper than smashing up your instruments, for sure, though perhaps a bit less of a Who-ish pop art statement.

On one memorable occasion during that first London winter we supported the Graham Bond Organisation at the Marquee. It was a pissing wet night. We did our set as usual, to reasonable acclaim. Then there was a gap. Ginger Baker hadn't arrived. Bond and Bruce came on, posing insouciantly as if this kind of stuff happened most nights, and started to play, drummerless. Then Ginger stormed on, glowering and livid, draped in a huge dripping black oilskin cape, toting a bunch of big nails and a hammer. As everyone including the audience cringed in terror, he furiously nailed his two bass drums to the floor, sat down behind the kit and joined in, still in his cape. A blinder.

Pitt, true to his word, bought us a van.

wikipedia

It was one of the very first Ford Transits, subsequently to become the transport of choice for gigging bands up and down the land. This was the stretch version, elongated wheelbase, double wheels at the back – just big enough to hold our kit and us. It was blue. Bob had acquired, from Hickies in Reading, a huge Hammond B3 and a Leslie (just the one), which took up more space than the band. We came up with a seating plan: driver and passenger in the front, three old bus seats salvaged from god knows where in a U formation behind, just about made eight. The job of driver was of course keenly contested, but this had to be hidden behind reluctance, as second prize was front seat passenger. A heavy emergency stop would probably have killed us all, impaled or crushed by Hammond, Fender or Ludwig. Andy promptly christened the van 'Bessie'. Bessie could have murdered a whole band.

I can't do an inventory of the gigs we played over this eighteen or so month period, nor would you wish to read one. Mainly because memory fails, of course, and I have neither the skills, time nor inclination to perform this kind of forensic reconstruction. But, also, because the ones I do recall are inextricably linked to certain girls, and I've already promised not to write just from that perspective. Shame really, some good tales – but they'd be told through a filter, how can you conceivably recall, never mind convey, the experience of those hot one-off encounters with girls from Letchworth or Nottingham or France? However, I am obliged to record some key history.

Soon after we hit London and acquired Bessie, we got a regular spot at Eel Pie Island, alternating with the Artwoods, sometimes on Sundays and sometimes Wednesdays. Eel Pie is now famous for having been Pete Townshend's corporate HQ, but back then it was just a decrepit 'hotel', which had miraculously retained an alcohol license. The playing space, with a remarkably copious stage, must once have been the hotel ballroom. Imagine that: in the Thirties, guests from around the World, America, South America, Germany, in skimpy diaphanous flapper frocks or baggy-trousered zoot suits, delivered by various cream and black motor carriages with huge headlights from Mayfair to the riverfront at Twickenham, and conveyed somehow across the narrow bridge, escorted delicately tripping over the neat lawn to the sumptuousness of the Eel Pie Island Ballroom, there to lindy-hop the night away to Ambrose or Geraldo… (Actually, research suggests that the bridge wasn't built until 1957, so prior to that guests were conveyed by boat, or possibly had to swim.)

It wasn't quite like that by the time we got there. The hotel was a wreck, I wouldn't have wanted to stay there even by my depleted standards. But the ballroom was still there, certainly, and Arthur Chisnall, who ran the gig, was highly organised. Two or three trips across the bridge, kit loaded on the back of his Mini flat-bed truck, quick set-up and we were ready to hit the bar, no draught beer so it was Newcastle Brown, by the neck. You could get some kind of bacon or sausage butty, which did for dinner. In winter, the hall was heated by industrial gas blowers, until the crowd arrived, when on a good night two or three hundred hot and hungry kids generated their own heat. We loved it, loved several of those hot female kids, got tanked on three or four Browns then went on and just did it. I remember having to go off for a piss halfway through a song, nobody noticed, Pete or Bob filled in for my solo – or perhaps the crowd thought this was just part of the act? In the summer, it was possible to take a stroll down by the river, across the strangely well-tended lawns, lie down on a grass bank with a suitable girl, discuss the different ways the leaves and other debris floated down through the Thames eddies…

Now, I recognise that everyone in the place apart from the band was stoned. Out of their skulls. Though perhaps with hindsight I recall Andy and Graham being absent for some time before we went on…? As for me, if I was even vaguely aware of the existence of drugs, I'd have been scared shitless of them. I'd read novels and tracts, I knew how marijuana could drive you insane and rot your brain. *Plus ca change…*

The Crom was the other important one.

The Cromwellian Club, at 3 Cromwell Road on the left-hand side heading west out of London towards, as it happened,

Bournemouth. We got a fairly regular Wednesday night residency, fifteen quid between us – not good money (we were getting £40 at Eel Pie), but that really didn't matter. What counted was being a house band in a regular hot spot.

This was the time of Swinging London, when for getting out and putting it about, if you felt you were on the scene, or should be, or wanted or craved to be, you had to be 'there'. There were several of these places – the Scotch of St James's, the Bag of Nails – all seedy and dirty by daylight (I assume from the Crom, never went to any of the others, mainly for financial reasons – a Coke could set you back five bob, the price of a good three or four pints in a normal pub), but at night lit by, infused in the reflected glow of the clientele. We never, as far as I recall, had any actual Beatles or Stones in on our Wednesdays, though Dylan showed once, at least we were told it was him; he lurked, head down, at a back table, surrounded by defenders, for an hour or so then vanished – now you see him, now you don't, maybe he was or wasn't there… but we did get a pretty good cross-section of the then B-list.

They listened – I remember catching Clapton's eye and raised eyebrow when I managed, probably by accident, a particularly snazzy multi-string hammer-on lick (the kind of stuff Hendrix would blow us all out with a few months later) during one of the bluesy solos which had become my trademark – but mostly, once we'd done our first set and they'd got mellow enough, they wanted to jam. Every week you could count on something happening. I don't want to make things up, so one clear distinctly recalled line-up will do: Stevie Winwood on organ, Eric Clapton on guitar, Keith Moon on drums, Long John Baldry singing, and our Billy gamely holding out on bass. The rest of us had been nudged off the stage.

I'd like to take this opportunity, by the way, of casting doubts on a story which I've been spreading around for the last forty years – that Eric Clapton played my Telecaster. I still have that guitar, but it stubbornly refuses to answer this question. Certainly he got up and plugged into my Fender amp; certainly he made a few adjustments to the amp settings and achieved his then definitive Buddy Guy sound; certainly I don't recall seeing him ship in his Les Paul or whatever he was using then (this was probably just on the cusp between Bluesbreakers and Cream)… I honestly don't remember for sure, and I'm certain he doesn't. His autobiography sheds no light.

I did however (I'm sure of this) use Andy Summers' plectrum. I dropped mine, couldn't find it, didn't have a spare, pleaded with Andy at the break – he went out to his car, found a little spare plec and delivered it to me just before we went back on, with a smile. Double hero! His autobiography also unaccountably overlooks this crucial event.

• • •

Back at Hutchings Walk, day to day life went on, just like any old suburban family. We sat out in the sheltered back garden, listening to Radios London and Caroline on our heavy old transistor radio. We did our best to get new numbers into the repertoire, taking tube trips down to Shepherds Bush to flip through the racks of 45s, Otis Redding, Sue label, picking up quite unsuitable ballady stuff but, occasionally, finding a gem like *Harlem Shuffle* – I'm certain as can be that we were the first band in Britain to perform this soul classic by Bob and Earl, I can sing the vocal backing as I type. A feature number was a slow blues called *Just Got Some*, by Willie Mabon (apparently covered, some time later, by Rod Stewart, though I can confidently say we got there first). I don't think I have to expound on the lyrics – but Dave Anthony would expound lasciviously on them, stretching out the innuendos from inches into yards.

At a gig at Southampton University, this number somehow expanded into near-infinity. Just occasionally, a performance does this – the band turns from eight individual blokes into a singularity, and spirals or plunges or swoops and dives through the music until it could go on forever: except that 'forever' entails the idea of 'time', which has, in fact, been temporarily abolished. On an unusual encouraging smiling nod from John, I played three rounds of the twelve bar solo, in F, rather than the usual two. Afterwards, we discovered that the whole brilliant gig had been taped by some local enthusiasts, who gladly played the tape back to us, and then gave it to us.

It's lost. Entrusted to various people over the next three years, this record, recording, of DAM at their very best – the band that briefly had the rest of them running scared – which would maybe have been the greatest live album of its time, up there with Georgie Fame at the Flamingo or Alex Harvey at the Star Club, just disappeared into some skip of negligence. I thought Graham had been the last custodian, and years later asked him if he still had it or knew where it might be. He didn't. I have never forgiven him for that drug induced carelessness. Ah well.

In the midwinter of 1966, some time in January, we got a return booking at the Disque a Go!Go! in Bournemouth, on a Wednesday night. We arranged it directly ourselves with Toni, no involvement from Pitt or London City; though Ken Pitt allowed it and waived his ten per cent, generously recognising our rights to nostalgia. We knew our way to the venue – but we hadn't accounted for access. We all had a lot more kit than the last time, especially Bob's massive B3. A certain amount of demolition had to take place before this huge organ could be got down the narrow stairway. I wondered at the time how Zoot and Graham Bond had managed this, and I still do. Years later I discovered the sawn-off split Hammond, which you could dismantle, transport and then put back together with a bit of alignment and a couple of wiring plugs, but this option almost certainly wasn't widely available when Bob bought his B3 – or maybe it was, and he consciously rejected it, purist that he was. (Earlier, he'd owned an old MG, a TD I think, which he unnecessarily stripped down then rebuilt over months, using a Haynes manual which he stole from Bournemouth Public Library under my name.) Certainly his Hammond was heavily customised by an organ fanatic, Ken Mundy, who lived in a terrace somewhere off Wimbledon Common, to no audible effect, at least to my ears.

But it didn't come in half. A door halfway down the stairs, and one side of its frame, had to be removed (and reinstated next day). But it didn't matter – this was our triumphant homecoming gig, local talent made bigtime, fresh from the Flamingo, the Marquee, all the fabled London hotspots, our loyal Bournemouth fanbase from the Saturday late-nighters showing up in droves. We were on £25 plus thirty per cent of the gate.

That afternoon, after we'd set up and done what's now called a soundcheck but then consisted in proving that the PA worked ('testing, testing, one two three, pah, pah, pah'), it started to snow. Within a couple of hours there were two or three inches on the roads. About twenty five people bravely turned up. Maria wasn't among them. Toni paid us our twenty five quid, mostly out of his own pocket. We never went back there again.

∙ ∙ ∙

We were steadily gigging, but then as now you really needed a record. Despite my on-going love of the medium, and my growing fascination with the process that ended up in that single squiggly spiral, I'd never been in a recording studio (apart from the basement studio of Ronaldson's Records, Southbourne, where Clem and me and the Sanderson Twins had recorded three tracks back in 1961 – I still have the unplayable acetate), and in fact had only the haziest concept of what went on there. So when Ken Pitt, at one of our regular progress meetings at Shepherds Market, announced that he'd secured a session at Abbey Road with the famous John Burgess, the Manfreds' producer (later to form AIR with George Martin), I went straight into my controlling leader mode. Obviously, first thing up would have to be a couple of songs, so I dredged my songwriting back catalogue – naturally assuming that our first hit would be self-penned, just like the Beatles or the Who.

I haven't talked about my songwriting. My first ever effort was called *I'll Walk Alone Until I Die*, an Elvis pastiche loosely from his post-Army Don Robinson period. Over the following years, I'd composed quite prolifically though almost always derivatively – Beatles, Stones, the Searchers, even Dylan, would spark off an idea in my mind and their idiom, which I would develop and claim, just to myself, as my own. I presented a couple to the Trackmarks, which could well have been their first single had I not left a month later. When I look back at some of those songs, actually, they stand up quite well, especially as the original triggers or influences would be a lot harder to detect now than then, except by pop journalists and musicologists. So maybe I can be the next Oasis…

But there wasn't much there for the Moods. In particular, there was nothing there for Dave Anthony. What he excelled at was throat-wrenching urban blues and soul, Ray Charles, Stax, Bobby Bland and so on, and I hadn't got round to emulating Percy Mayfield or Isaac Hayes in my writing. We didn't want to go down the road of covering obscure soul records by obscure US artists – we wanted original material which was going to hit them between the eyes. I couldn't provide it.

The best I could come up with was a recent teen-angst song called *Give It A Chance*, with quite a good hook based on an old four-chord trick (A-D, E-G), and a rather hackneyed lyric prompted by, I think, being dumped by an actress called Natasha – Pete, who took an interest in my writing, told me he thought it was heartfelt. I worked it up, doubling the chorus, adding in call-and-response horn parts, refining the tune to fit Tony's vocal style, and scoring a punchy brass break (melodically and harmonically quite unrelated to the original song, it could probably have been expanded into a separate hit, or at least a chorus, in its own right). We played the finished product to Burgess, who opined that it was a good B side (time has passed its judgement on that).

Meanwhile, Manfred Mann and Mike Hugg had penned, and demoed, a song called *New Directions*, a stab at catching the crest of the early Sixties zeitgeist. They obviously didn't feel it was suitable for the Manfreds, and were in any case too busy with *Pretty Flamingo*. So in about February, they handed it in to Ken, who handed it down to us.

We listened. It didn't sound like a Moods song (any more than *Give It A Chance* had). But it was the only one we had, and the famous John Burgess had been hooked and temporarily booked. A three hour session was available at Abbey Road, subject to us having two songs in more or less live-recordable condition. Three hours was the norm in those days. (The whole of the Beatles' first album was recorded in four or five such sessions.) You had to enter the studio with a rehearsed product – the producer would then work his magic, in three hours, to turn it into that ineluctable, irresistible squiggly groove that would eventually seep out of tinny speakers across the land and somehow spark, in a million souls, that lust which had sent me down to Bourne Radio, all those years ago, in the snow, for Elvis's *One Night*.

Well, for this to happen something drastic needed to be done to this song. I have got the original demo. It's pretty bland, all tinkly piano and strummed guitar. We somehow saw that dynamics, light and shade, was the key. I must have been listening to Gil Evans or some such thing, because the brass chord intro to *New Directions* is pretty far out for 1966 pop. I'm still proud of that piece of scoring. In fact, I still find it difficult to deconstruct. There are, I know, only three notes in there, because we only had three horns and there certainly was neither the time nor, for us, the technology for overdubbing – but which three notes precisely? I reckon, in the key of C, bottom up: C, G flat, B flat; you try it! If this is correct, this may be one of the first-ever deliberate uses of the tritone – the diabolic interval, the flattened fifth – in mainstream pop music. (I exclude 'West Side Story', which is mostly written around the thing, and is where I discovered it.)

Anyway, be that as it may, it was a dramatic kick which achieves a lot: it sets the dynamic scene, nudging the listener into what's coming, reflects the thrust of the title and the lyric (this was in fact a new direction, once we'd dumped half of Mann/Hugg's original words), and grabs your ears by their lugs.

Dave Anthony's Moods

Once the song gets going, Dave's voice takes control, cracking exactly when it should; Bill's bass solidly underpins (apart from the famous fluff in the coda), whilst John's drum fills are uncharacteristically wild and vibrant. Bob's Hammond breaks, mixed in at just the right moments, are perfect. And my guitar riff (from the original Mann-Hugg demo) holds it all together, until the bridge where I cut loose in my best Pete Townshend mode. Then, when you expect a fade, instead we end with a swelling affirmative C major chord, with hissing cymbals. Pretty damn good, I still say.

• • •

Before that, early in 1966, Ken Pitt had come up with a lucrative scheme. A New York American woman called Goldie had had a minor hit, with her group the Gingerbreads, a song called *Can't You Hear My Heartbeat*. I have to confess I can't remember a note of it, and thank the lord we weren't asked to play it. Goldie was branching out into this new R&B thing and, England being the coming breeding ground and marketplace for all and every new kind of music, she had come over here, all New York brass and insecurity. We were contracted to be Goldie's backing band for a two-month tour. She was brash, intimidating, unattainably desirable. I fell in love with her, but that obviously wasn't going to happen.

A couple of professional notes about Goldie, which I might as well slot in here. 1) She asked me to write her a song, which had to be called *Messing Up My Mind*, which I did. (Sample lyric 'Don't close your eyes, like you're closing them now'.) It didn't get used, fortunately. 2) She recorded a great version of *Going Back*, briefly released on Immediate, only to have it turned down by Goffin/King and withdrawn because she'd foolishly (and detrimentally) altered the lyrics without permission. The Moods subsequently used this arrangement as the basis for a high spot of our live set – but never had the nous to record it! Dusty Springfield, of course, had the rather bland hit.

The deal was that we would do a truncation of our usual set (Dave singing), take a short break, then Goldie would come on and blow the crowd away. The first booking for this formula was at the Marquee in Wardour Street, about as prestigious as they come. We were obviously meant to play it low key in our own set, then cut loose for the fabulous Goldie. Well, that might have been a good plan had we been told about it. But the music press were there, the first time ever at a DAM gig. So we cut loose in our own set. I quote Chris Welch's Melody Maker Review, February 12 1966, in full:

"*A cheering if sparse crowd greeted Goldie at her Marquee stint last week. Bright and cheerful, she soon had her supporters swinging, backed by a tremendous group, Dave Anthony's Moods.*

"*Earlier, Dave roared through his own powerful set, and a whole lot of groups are going to get a serious shock when they hear the Moods in action.*

"*Dave is an excellent singer, with a good range, and a total absence of shrieking, which is often mistaken for blues feel. With a line up of trumpet, trombone, tenor, organ, guitar, bass guitar and drums, the band at times developed Ted Heathian power. Manfred, Zoot, Georgie and the Animals – watch out!*"

(Here's a montage of the original report, made at the time by Ken's secretary, with her own annotations.)

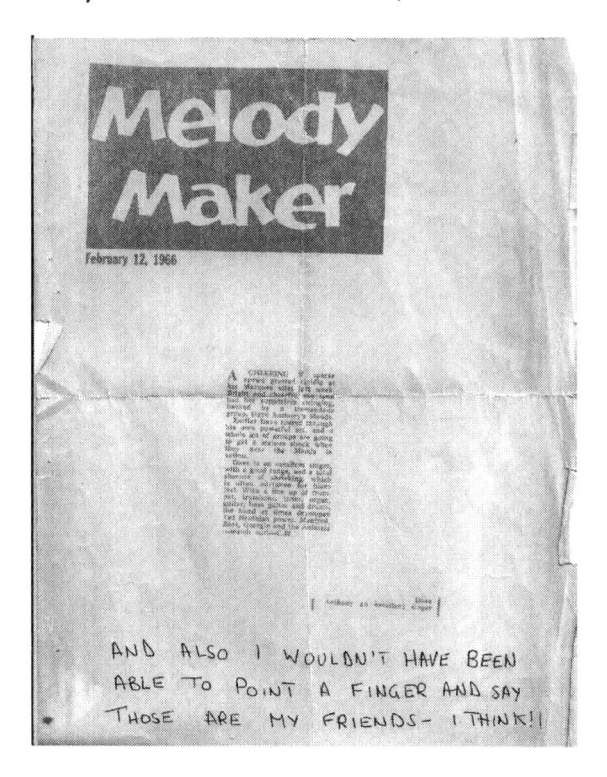

A few glosses might be relevant. The 'sparse' crowd consisted of about fifty people, hardly enough to populate the bar area. The weather, as seemed always to be the case when we had a big gig, was atrocious. Ted Heath was a big-band leader of the fifties, still active in the sixties but easily confused with the leader of the Tory party and erstwhile prime minister; the reference was doubtless well meant, but I at least found it cringingly embarrassing – we were trying to be cutting edge, for God's sake, not some kind of throwback. And the last sentence's warning to the superstars of the day was, to say the least, damaging. Not for the last time, the opposition would be out to get us.

Nevertheless, it was critical acclaim of a sort. Ken Pitt failed completely to capitalise on this, or on the release of *New Directions* in April. We finished the Goldie tour, mostly of US airbases in Norfolk – Andy has reminded of me of one horrifying date, at somewhere called Brownhills. They'd never seen a trombone before, and Graham, rather recklessly, played to this ignorance by dipping his slide down off the edge of the stage at the mob and making low farting trombone noises, until some smartarse girl managed to grab it, causing some damage, whereupon we cut our losses and walked off, undignifiedly dragging our kit behind us and escaping to the van without managing to collect the balance of our £25 fee. Bob inadvisably spat in the promoter's face, earning Andy a split lip. I think broken glass was involved in there too.

We went into the studio with Goldie – Pye, off the Edgware Road – and made what Andy considers to be our best records: a red hot version of Bobby Bland's *Turn On Your Lovelight*; a number called *Think About The Good Times* (which can be found on the internet), both with backing vocals by Madeleine Bell and Kiki Dee; and a couple of sides for Island, under the pseudonym Patsy Cole, one of which was a lugubrious eight-bar doo-wop blues called *Disappointed Bride*, on which Pete played a brilliantly sleazy sax solo and I did a pretty snaky guitar obligato.

The person who posted *Disappointed Bride* on YouTube claims that the backing was by people like Georgie Fame or maybe Stevie Winwood, Spencer Davis etc., and that the recording was an 'extra' at the tail end of some unspecified session on which Goldie was singing background. They're wrong. This is the Moods (sans Dave Anthony of course), at their very best. (Andy recalls that Chris Blackwell brought in his own bass player, which meant that Bill didn't play on these sides, much to his chagrin.) Goldie's own recollections are fuzzy – she remembers a session with Winwood and Davis, but not with the Moods, which is obviously wrong – but I stand by the above.

New Directions came out on 22 April. Unbelievably, we were too stupid to include it in our live set (and our manager too detached to advise, or force us to do so). I think we played it live just once, at Swadlincotes Miner's Club or some such place, to blank beer-fuelled oblivion from an entirely male crowd of Derbyshire oiks, to whom the music was no more than a necessary racket of an excuse to get roaring bladdered and have a good old laugh, largely at the expense of this rather weird-looking musical bunch. It wasn't the best way of promoting our first hit single.

Why did, or didn't, we do it? Unless you were the Beatles or the Stones, the only ways to sell a record were to play it live and get it on the radio. We did neither. Why we didn't play it live I'll never know, though it actually wouldn't have made that much difference given the number and spread of our gigs at the time. (I think it sold well in Chippenham.) Radio play was another matter, and I blame the lack of this full-square on our manager,

Kenneth Pitt. To get a record on the radio then, you needed to exercise your contacts – wine and dine them, blackmail them if possible, fuck them literally or figuratively, but above all have them. Pitt didn't have any. Which is strange, considering his prominence in the Mayfair gay underground scene, also frequented by more than one prominent DJ of the time.

To be slightly fair, the only options were Luxembourg and the two Pirates, Caroline and Radio London. The BBC was a no-go, and TV hardly existed unless you were already up there. Luxembourg had of course been going for decades, and was where I got a lot of my 1950s inside knowledge. (Other boys were tucked up in bed when I was meticulously research-surfing on that 'wave of phase', picking up on Ray Charles and other early Atlantic stuff from Jack Jackson, whose Decca Record Show featured the London American label and others in 1959.) The Pirates had been broadcasting for a year or two and were illegal but thriving, the only ones we listened to once we managed to track down their medium wavelengths on Bob's early tranny.

Pitt got us one play on Luxembourg. We were told roughly when it was going to come on, about ten on a Saturday night. For some forgotten reason I was outside a pub in Corfe Castle, Dorset, with my brother and a forgotten girl or two. We tuned a radio in to 208, and sure enough *New Directions* came on. The DJ talked over the intro, and faded it before the bridge. That was it, the entire extent of promotion of this great record. (Although my brother reckons it was also played a bit on Radio London.) It sold about 500.

(Eighteen months or so later, in Italy, I received through the post a letter from Ken Pitt, enclosing a cheque for about £5 as composer's royalties for *Give It A Chance*. The letter suggested that I endorse the cheque by signing it on the back, thereby making it payable to whoever happened to have it in their hands, something you could, unbelievably now, do in those days, and send it back to him to be set against the Mood's debts to him. I thought: fuck you, and banked it.)

• • •

In April 1966, Pete Sweet, unsurprisingly really given the gut-ripping stresses he must have been under – his passionate commitment to the music versus his day job running a B&B by remote control, via his wife – reluctantly told us that he had to give it up. He'd be able to hang on long enough for us to find a replacement, assuming weeks rather than months. I've said nearly enough about Pete, his musical skill and enthusiasm and broad-mindedness – though his heart was in love with Humphrey Lyttelton, his joy of just getting up there and blowing would have led him down whatever roads opened up (he engaged with every genre and sub-genre we ever leant towards, however outré) and DAM just happened to open up for him, for a while. I hope he enjoyed it. An extraordinary man. The last time I saw him, in the late eighties, he was back to playing 'mainstream trad' with Graham in pubs around Poole.

This was the very early, unsighted, beginning of the start of the end.

We advertised in the Melody Maker for a professional horn player to be employed on salary, about £30 a week I think, which meant we had to make about £150 to feed ourselves and break even. No professional economists or nitpickers should question or connive at these purely illustrative numbers; the point is merely that the employed sax man would be soaking up an inordinate proportion of our net income. In theory, Pitt should have been doing the books, but I have no memory of him ever, ever asking those sorts of questions. I wasn't much engaged with that money stuff. Bill had somehow got appointed as our in-house accountant; he kept records of ins and outs and doled out the residue of each gig, pro rata, to each of us. (I have a feeling that the need for this role arose at one of our group meetings, somebody said 'can anyone do maths?', I kept my mouth and my O level distinction shut, and Bill Jacobs dumbly said something like 'um…', and got the job. As it turned out, he did it very efficiently, as you'll see.)

I can't remember if we got more than one reply to the MM advert, but there was certainly only one that qualified – Bob Downes. He came up to Hutchings Walk for an audition. I think we were all a bit in awe of this unknown professional, with an impressive track record (The John Barry Seven) and, as we soon discovered, a masterly technique. We tried out a few numbers, including my stripped-down chart for our show-opener *Walk on the Wild Side*. Back in 65 I had sat down with the whole band and worked them through Oliver Nelson's amazing arrangement, converting a full big-band into just five lead parts, guitar, organ, trumpet, trombone, sax. Somehow between us we had distilled the essence of the piece, complete with the deliberate horn discords in the break (which I assigned to each different voice, just to keep them on their toes). It was pretty good. (Certainly better than the Artwoods' feeble effort, with which they once tried to upstage us at Eel Pie.) Now, looking back, I realise that when the transition from big-band to organ came, we should have all walked off the stage except John, Bill, and of course Bob M, who'd have unleashed a lethal organ trio which could've lasted the whole set (and also given the rest of us a piss break).

Downes, in these circumstances, did more than well. We were probably hard on him – a new foster-brother – but as I said we were probably scared of him. He's told me that, actually, he was a bit scared of us, something I'd never have imagined at the time... so we all probably got into some kind of double-bind feedback loop, within the first ten minutes, which never got completely unravelled over the next nine months.

Obviously, we took him on. There were complexities in the deal, including having to pick him up at the Hanger Lane Giratory for North-facing gigs – not the easiest of tasks, if you've ever been there – but he was the right man for the job, as well as the only one. Pete gave us the nod, which was good enough for me. After we'd all shaken hands on the deal (I wonder why we didn't go down the pub? Probably it was the afternoon and they didn't open till seven), Downes asked one fateful question:

"Do you guys smoke?"

As most of us had lighted fags in our fingers at the time, some of us exchanged perplexed glances; I may even have said something dumb like "well obviously..." Andy and Graham, however, exchanged a meaningful glance. I think Andy may have made some kind of 'no, but...' response – certainly further meaningful glances were exchanged. Pete Sweet said "don't you guys go smoking no shit, mind", possibly with a hint of a wink.

There followed what must have been some pretty brief and intensive handover rehearsal sessions: so much so that, he tells me, on his first gig Downes, having been seated in the back of the van and so unable to lock onto faces, found himself being chatted to at the bar by some guy who eventually introduced himself as our organist, Bob M. Clearly, we were still working fast and hard then.

Even before this first personnel change, a catalyst, old Pete's calming avuncular influence replaced by Bob Downes' hip professional go-for-it, tensions in the band had been festering. My relationship with Tony had more or less broken down. In some rehearsal session, on some point of detail about just precisely when I felt he should come back in, he blew up and yelled "I'm not going to be told what to do by some fucking two-bit guitar player!" Bob M was withdrawn, trying to extract himself from a horrible girl called Heather (my brother also narrowly escaped that one). Graham's marriage was gently eroding. Andy regularly vanished, like some ghost from another sphere. John was taken for granted by all, a drummer. He'd get drunk and pour it all out, inarticulately, but no-one was listening.

A couple of weeks after Bob Downes joined, at a gig in some provincial town, let's call it Leicester, Andy sidled up to me. "There's a bloke here. We can get some stuff if we want."

"Stuff?"

"You know... Two quid each."

It was a difficult question. I was aware of the existence of drugs by now, had smelt strange aromas in the back room at the Flamingo, and perhaps even been secondarily influenced by them. I was hearing music, live and recorded, which I didn't understand, which could only ever have been done by means of some superior power, which of course could only mean drugs. At the same time, I must have been indoctrinated somehow into believing in the putative evils, terrified. How? Well, there was no such thing as 'the media' in those days, not in the way we recognise it now as an influence; in any case I had a healthy disrespect for the Express (the only paper that came into the house, mainly so we could collaboratively do the square 9 letter rebus word game – make as many words as you can out of DIMENSION); the actual content of the newspaper was disdainfully dismissed, if noticed. We didn't watch much TV, but nonetheless knew that its content was even more vacuous and irrelevant.

So it can only have been my timidity holding me back. I'd thought I'd got over that, had certainly lost the shyness. This was an important tipping point, but the key memory of how I reached that decision is lost and gone. I just said "yeah, OK".

There was an unspoken consensus that the Leicester band room probably wasn't the best location for some of us to lose our drug virginity. So a few days later we assembled at Hutchings Walk for the great pot experiment. Bob Michaels and Tony Head had opted out. Andy, Graham and Bob D were the experts. Bill, John and me were by now avidly fearful or fearfully expectant. It was a bit like a séance. (Funnily enough, a few months previously Bob M had set up just such an event, where we all sat round the table watching him manoeuvre an upturned glass round a table, conjuring up messages from the depths of his imagination of our desires...)

Downes skinned up. He was actually a non-smoker, so quite rightly got huffy when I balked at providing the tobacco from one of my precious Woodbines... but two joints eventually got built and smoked by the six of us. It certainly tasted good. "Mmm," I thought, then "is 'mmm' a sufficiently meaningful response to this nice tasting cigarette? Better write this down, deconstruction of the mmm response, so find some paper, oh and a pen; pencil will do fine, not a problem... though there is significant difference, or should that be dichotomy, whatever one of those is (*laughs out loud at this point*) between pencils and pens, better note that... trouble is brain is going faster than fingers or hands, so impossible to get all this stuff down before it evaporates... I need some kind of dictation machine..."

After half an hour or day of this sort of crap, I stumbled across John's acoustic guitar. Oh yeah, of course, I thought, play. Picked it up, started some kind of vamp. Next thing I knew my left hand fingers were flying all over the place – I didn't seem to be able to keep them down from the top end of the fretboard, somehow my hand just kept whizzing up there. Eventually I regained some kind of control over what I was doing, and began to apply my customary analysis. The music is happening in my brain, not in my fingers; but it can only be made by my fingers. So we need to get the signal down that long neurological route from head to hand. Does this stuff somehow short-circuit that path? At this moment, I think so...

Many improvisatory musicians will concur, I suspect, with that. So, to the extent that what you have to play has to be improvised, dope is without question a great aid, a terabit hyperlink through the various relevant synapses. Whether it's equally effective in enhancing other more protracted, non-real-time mental processes, creative or otherwise, is harder to call. Opinions (mine included) differ.

•••

Summer 1966. Eel Pie; Cromwellian; 100 Club; away trips up North (we actually played at Leeds University once, I needed new strings and found my way to exactly the right City centre music shop, to my gratification, not to say astonishment; the place seemed to have changed a lot in three years). We usually came back from the Midlands (Brum, Nottingham) the same night, stopping at the Blue Boar (officially known as Watford

Gap Services) on the M1 for 2 a.m. fry-ups and encounters with other similarly destitute, knackered musicians.

Bear in mind, if you will, that bands at our level didn't have the services of those beasts of burden, logistics engineers and psychiatric counsellors called 'road managers'. We did it all ourselves. A typical first time Saturday away gig at let's call it The Cave in Bromsgrove, would go roughly as follows:

1. Wake up, get dressed and if lucky washed and shaved.
2. Hopefully the van is already loaded with the gear, ready to roll. I make sure my Telecaster is in the van, not the bedroom.
3. Elect driver, head north, picking up Downes at Hanger Lane, make sure he's remembered his sax. If he's also scored, smoke a joint for the M1/M45.
4. Find the Cave (how did we do that the first time? No satnav: not sure we even had a map).
5. Check out the Cave, making sure we can get the B3 through the door/down or upstairs; don't forget the Disque. Hump gear into the Cave (I learnt everything I know, which is a lot, about how to carry heavy square boxes), set it up.
6. Sound test ('yeah, all seems to work'), find a pub. Turn up in time to play.
7. Play.
8. Disconnect and hump gear back out of Cave, making sure it's not left unattended. (At one early Marquee gig, Bill had left his beautiful white Fender Jazz bass leaning unwatched against a wall for about two minutes. He got a nice Precision replacement though, pre-owned by Jack Bruce.)

9. Drive or be driven back to London, via Blue Boar grease-out.

10. Fall into bed. If lucky, sleep.

On the subject of our equipment and its precariousness, at one gig in Guildford, while we were humping the gear out, an enthusiastic boy offered to help me carry Bob's Hammond. Unthinkingly I said "OK". Halfway out of the hall, he dropped his end – I couldn't control mine and the thing crashed to the floor, keyboard down. Bob dashed up. I think there were tears. The keys were all over the place – this magnificent instrument, his pride and joy, seemed to have been trashed by a moment of carelessness or incompetence (both mine; I can't blame the unwitting helper).

Analyst Tim took over: "OK, let's get home, then we'll sort this out". None of the numbed people argued, not even Bob; so I got that one right. Next day, the organ seemed, perhaps by the relaxing vibrations of Bessie's trip back up the A3, to have righted itself to some extent. Bob and I had a look inside it. I could see how some links between the keys and the switches had come loose, and how to reconnect them. The Hammond's technology combines a lever, the key you press, with a switch, the circuitry which feeds through to the sound modulation system controlled by the stops and drawbars. (I think that's about right – experts please correct me, I haven't done any research.) Bob and I spent a whole day doing this. Once we'd achieved and tested this, I think I earned his long-standing gratitude, and resentment.

Back at Hutchings Walk, the weird domesticity carried on. Once Pete had gone, the sleeping arrangements became slightly more civilised, two or three rather than four to a room. Tony, Anna and their two-year-old boy, David, had one to themselves, obviously. There was a cat somewhere in there too. I got a proper bed to replace the fold-up I'd had before. We took it in turns to cook, without any formally imposed rota. Anna, Italian matriarch-in-waiting, occasionally took over and set us on cleaning or cooking or gardening fatigues, which we mostly accepted with well-faked good grace. I've already mentioned the great World Cup Final fiasco. Musically we were ticking over – no great demand on us to produce anything new or original, the regular dates wanted same again, the one-off away ones didn't know we were just going through well-tried motions. Money was gradually getting better. You will have noticed a pattern to my life as I've described it so far – a longish spell of calm, then a violent churn, followed by a long tail-off into the next cycle, repeat several times, or forever.

Tragedy

It's about 8 a.m., early for us. I'm woken up by voices outside the bedroom. Tony, Anna, others. Another of those domestic rows. I turn over, try to let myself drop back into sleep (shut it out), but the voices get louder. I can't ignore them any longer. I sit up and see that John and Graham are up, gone. Something's going on, but nobody's called me. I have to get up. As I swing out of bed, I hear an unfamiliar voice. I somehow know it's a doctor.

"He's been dead for hours."

• • •

I don't know what the inquest verdict was. It fell into the class later defined as 'cot death', although David had apparently been up and about, unsupervised, playing with his mother's make-up for ages, but this was ruled out as a cause. The funeral was in Bournemouth a few days later. The band all attended, all appropriately dressed. How did I get hold of a dark suit? I know I did. Must have been borrowed, from my father perhaps. My mother chose and sent flowers.

Straight afterwards, an angry Anna told me, me! that it was our fault. There was no arguing with that – you can always assign blame for anything tragic to anyone, and who's in a position to dispute? I don't think it was our, or my, fault – but you can't counter grief, can you?

She also told me, less acceptably, that Tony wasn't doing this anymore. He'd left. He'd disappeared. None of us got the chance to talk to him. This landed us with a bit of a problem.

Carrying On

My memory is unreliable. We need to agree upon this point, so that I can continue to write this. The next few days were a blur. We had a gig, a committed unbreakable date, at Leatherhead R&B Club. Pitt rose to the occasion. He had an up and coming young singer, Davie Jones, just about to be rebranded, who could help us out for this one gig. I'm fairly sure that we rehearsed with him – he knew all the numbers, was bouncy and enthusiastic – what I don't remember is whether he actually got up with us at Leatherhead. Isn't that pathetic? Well, not really, back then this guy was just another singer, albeit an obviously unusual one, who'd made it clear that he wasn't interested in joining full time (or Pitt told him not to, having other ambitions for David, the next Anthony Newley), but would be happy to help us out, as a one-off, in our hour of need. My rubbish memory can't help out here. I'd like to imagine or pretend that it did happen, though it almost certainly didn't. I probably stepped in as emergency vocalist. David, are you there?

This is one point at which the band probably should have split. 'Dave Anthony's Moods' without Dave Anthony doesn't make a lot of sense. Dave Anthony's Moods without the fire, focus and confidence of the Bournemouth days makes even less, and I'd detected auspices of that degeneration more or less straight after Pete left. A certain sloppiness was creeping in: solos repeated by rote, important grace notes missed; tempos speeding up. We weren't getting better. We weren't getting worse either, true. We were much the same.

I don't think the thought of breaking up the band crossed anyone's mind. Certainly not mine. As I have told, I conduct my life on a succession of single tracks, serial squiggly grooves from which I don't jump of my own accord but can only be jolted, booted or nudged from by some external force, some quantum stumbling in and knocking over the record player. If, for example, Bowie had said "let's write songs together", I'd have jumped without looking down. But no jolt happened.

Clearly, we needed a singer, and there was no way it was going to be me.

The Cheynes were a minor R&B outfit I had seen once or twice – I remember a good guitarist, Phil Sawyer, who a bit later became famous with Spencer Davis. I certainly don't remember their singer. I remember the Mark Leeman Five slightly better, but not much. Anyway, Mark Leeman himself died in June 66 and was replaced by the singer from The Cheynes, Roger Peacock. The group kept its name, but must have broken up, because just when we needed a singer, Roger became available, and Ken Pitt somehow picked him up. Those last four words are carefully chosen. The Cheynes apparently became notorious for a homoerotic sequence in some forgotten pop film compilation, and I can cast Peacock in that, I think.

I disliked him at first sight. At second sight, I was charmed. At third, my usual rational resolution kicked in – live with what you have. Roger was blessed or damned with his immaculately appropriate surname. He preened and posed, alternately exposing then concealing himself. He had a lovely smile, and a nasty scowl. He came to a rehearsal and knew most of the songs, was up for the ones he didn't know, like Eddie Holland's *Leaving Here* (a rare early Motown stormer at the time, long before Motörhead got their hands on it), up and ready to roll.

He was also an enthusiastic pothead, of the dangerous sort. I had, by now, come to use cannabis primarily as a playing aid, secondarily as a short cut to a rather indiscriminate version of creative process. In both cases, the key was unwavering focus – when I was doing this, or this, it was all I was doing, totally excluding anything else. We have all been there, obsessing over a teabag, or a couple of stars in the sky, for as long as it takes to get distracted (oh, the anguish of forever losing that sharp unique point of focus), or fall asleep. In the deep heights of this state, I once wrote *I never want to be any other way*, It was all and only about me.

Roger Peacock, by contrast, felt that drugs were about risk. He used them as a route to misconceived adventure – dragging me out to the depths of his shady West End milieu, forcing me to pretend I'd partaken of dangerous games (I was once made to recount, to the other guys, some details of an orgy at George Harrison's flat, which certainly never took place, I'd have remembered that). I played along, of course, easier than not. The real trouble was, this attitude extended to the music.

Roger was a lazy singer. He didn't think he had to learn the lyrics, never mind interpret them. OK, to be fair, not many songs in our repertoire demanded that much interpretation – *Shout, Shotgun,* even *Poppa's Got a Brand New Bag* weren't that subtle. But even when there was something to be said, you could tell that, actually, his performance was more about him than about the song. One of the greatest soul songs ever, Otis Redding's *I've Been Loving You Too Long*, despite all the lyric's nuances of ambiguity and sexual insecurity, became a self-pitying mumble, evolving to a screaming climax to which the Moods of course gleefully applied their blasting power, stretching it out to two or three minutes. (Making the songs last longer was one lazy way of avoiding having to learn new ones. We didn't see it that way at all, of course. We were being cutting-edge.)

For a short time that autumn, Roger and Bob M cooked up a plan whereby we'd all wear outrageous make-up and perform some kind of onstage 'happening', the music being merely the soundtrack to ill-conceived amateur dramatics. Thankfully, this didn't last long in the face of sullen compliance from the rest of us (and outright contemptuous refusal from Bob Downes). The time and place for that would of course come along, when Arthur Brown launched his crazy world and, a few years later, Bowie's reinventions changed popular music for ever; but Dave Anthony's Moods were never going to blaze that particular trail.

To me, that stuff was pitiful. Songs – I still believe this – are a crossover between two major time-based art forms, music and poetry, and as such are due total undiluted respect. Especially if you're a singer – it's your duty to interpret that relationship to the utmost degree of perfection. At its best, this art form, song, combines the essentials of each of its several components in such a way that none of them can stand alone. Melody, harmony, rhythm and words – story – become inseparable. Once achieved, the trick seems easy, but it requires the craft of the singer. Roger Peacock had that craft, but a lot of the time he lazily, negligently or wilfully misused it.

Meanwhile, gigs continued to come in fairly steadily. Opportunities were also thrown our way. We auditioned as Eric Burdon's new band, to no avail. I vaguely recall a few others of that kind. We backed Kenny Lynch once, at the London Hilton. We played our habitual circuit of reliable West Country and Midlands venues, with their reliable attendances and loyal boys and girls. Once again, the moment at which I should have ducked out came and went, drained away by my inertia.

We were auditioned, in another Pitt deal, by one Doctor Arango, for an eight week residency at the Piper Club in Milan, Italy, on a fixed wage of the lire equivalent of about £40 a month each – each! – unheard-of money. This sounded pretty good. I think I picked up, from conversations with Ken Pitt, asides and evasions, that this was our exit strategy, as it's now called.

Somewhere in there, in reaction to some inflated misdemeanour born of mutual dislike or incompatibility, we sacked or were sacked by Bob Downes. John was tasked with breaking the news to him, in the van after the tipping-point transgression and a hasty band conference which must have been just confirmation of an existing, unvoiced consensus, or cabinet conspiracy. John was excruciatingly long-winded, everyone including Downes was cringing with embarrassment by the time he'd managed to come to the point. Bob took it very well, really, having already (he told us) secured a gig touring with the Soul Sisters in a couple of weeks. We decided to carry on as a seven-piece, just the two horns.

Shotgun, a one-chord instrumental riff by Junior Walker and the All-stars with a meaningless and largely superfluous lyric, had been part of our set for some time. We'd structured our version around the original single, as a sax solo feature for Pete and then Bob. Once we'd dispensed with a sax player, the natural thing would have been to drop the number, but instead I took over the solo role on guitar. Improvising on a single chord and riff can be a bit demanding, not to say tedious, for me as well as the rest of the band. So we allowed *Shotgun* to develop into an extended group improvisation, which eventually could last forever. I'd do a few of the customary cliché-licks, then back away, catch somebody's eye and ear with, say, an E minor seventh arpeggio, which might get taken up by John with some ride cymbal bell tinkles; then Bob might come in with a bit of Bach or Tatum, and Andy and Graham would make strange shifting chords, off in a key of their own. It grew each time we played it, never in the same direction. Once, at some theatre gig in Blackpool, where we had a half-hour slot, we did just this one number, for half an hour. I wonder now what the audience made of it.

• • •

Christmas Eve 1966. We were double booked by the Gunnells – the Ram Jam in Brixton for the early session, then the Flamingo All-Nighter, midnight through to four or five. Nobody wanted to do this. I'm blaming Roger for the half-baked plot that ensued. Five of us connived to get out of the Flamingo gig. (We didn't tell Bob because, we agreed, he might spill the beans, still having some vestige of moral, not to say common, sense).

The plot was: on the way out of the Ram Jam after the set, a volunteer actor would be stricken with, let's say, appendicitis and have to be rushed off to hospital, in Bournemouth. Therefore we couldn't do the gig. Everyone would sympathise, wish the poor victim well, muddle through without us. John got the job – well, the drummer's the most indispensable, isn't he? So, coming down the iron steps out of the Ram Jam, John would suddenly collapse, clutching his belly. Concerned colleagues would rush to the rescue, gather him up and ease him and his agony into the van (which would of course already have been packed). We'd then race off to Bournemouth and some kind of happy Christmas, of which I remember nothing.

The acting was impeccable: but it didn't fool Johnny Gunnell. What were we thinking of? To imagine that we could get away with casually dumping this massive unsolvable problem on London's most powerful gangster-based music control organisation? I now feel quite sorry for them, committed as they were to supplying live all-night music to a heavingly full Flamingo, a crowd with high expectations and high regard for this band, and all of these people to be let down at the twelfth hour by the arrogant whim of a bunch of self-important idiots – stupid is the only word that fits. Shame and anger often go together; in this case, looking back, they're fused into a single emotion for which I don't have a word. I regret my connivance at this fraud: especially as it proved to be the next step towards the decay and collapse of the Moods.

I reckon this was the tipping point for Ken Pitt. I've been critical of his managerial and promotional skills and commitment whilst he had charge of us, and I stand by that, but he was a decent man and we gave him a hard time. If nothing else, he did bring money (and so by implication commitment) to the table, whereas we brought nothing but our unshakeable self-belief, founded or not, accompanied by not a lot of actual music. But he should not have been expected to protect us from our own dumb arrogance, and he didn't.

Coincidentally or not, early in January the Arango deal was hastily confirmed. Doctor Arango turned out to be a middleman acting for a Milanese impresario called Leo Wachter. Leo had brought the Beatles to Italy for three gigs in 1965, had since been promoting a few local sub-Beatle groups, also Italian solo singers, had not much idea about actual music but knew that the first English band to hit Milan at a local level would be, well, something – I don't believe his thinking went any deeper than that. We knew nothing of any of this at the time, of course. It just looked like a great opportunity, good money, foreign adventure.

We convinced ourselves, somehow, that being shipped off to this faraway land of which we knew virtually nothing was going to be our big break. Actually, we convinced each other. It was a conspiracy of noise. The more one person talked it up, the harder it became for anyone else to express queasy misgivings if they had such things; I certainly did, and I think so did everyone. On this occasion, though, I didn't have a get-out. I was in deep enough that alternatives to music didn't even cross the little that was left of my rational mind: I was in this thing, no other options existed. So I had to stick with the Moods, and the Moods were going to Italy, because no-one was able to say 'no we're not'.

Over the last few weeks, we pumped the hubris up to steam heat. We got new state-of-the-trend stage suits: mine included an aquamarine velvet knee length coat with five buttons (sadly no detailed pictures of this survive), plus two satin shirts, one green, one cream, with collars like spaniel's ears. I think I gave the jacket to Graham later, but I kept the shirts for years.

I got one of the first fuzz boxes, a red stick-like thing that you plugged into the guitar and then into the amp, enabling me to sound a bit like the *Satisfaction* riff. (I took it to show Ken Mundy, Bob's organ guru in Wimbledon, for some reason; he opened it up and carefully noted the circuitry.)

Bill and I needed new amps; no way would our little Fenders cut it against this suddenly inflated self-image. We needed 100 watt Marshall stacks. We tried to negotiate a deal with Don Strike, and were sent away with fleas in our ears, or at least in mine, quite rightly as I'd been reneging on hire purchase payments on the Fender for months. John's mother came to what seemed to be the rescue, with some sort of financing package which I, for one, never heard any details of – was it a gift? A loan? An investment? I didn't ask, didn't really wonder. The Marshall fairy had landed. We crept back to Strike, perhaps with a smidgeon of schadenfreude, and offered him the deal, no hard feelings etc. It didn't take him very long to calculate the value of his principles. The amps were delivered within days. We had to work out a whole new way of loading Bessie.

There was a lot of admin, things which the vestiges of responsibility in me insisted on. Mr Adlard had to be given notice – I remember how difficult this was, for some reason, and how weeks later I had to conduct a diplomatic correspondence with him, something to do with offsetting an overpaid month's rental against the undoubtedly significant cost of cleaning the place; a point which that good man graciously took, and waived any residual balance that might have remained in his favour. I had to be fast on my feet to renew my driving licence: I'd been running on empty for two years, and we all had to get an International Driving Licence, a strange multi-page document which, as far as I can recall, contained absolutely no information except that we possessed a British driving licence, in several languages. (One of these would come in handy a couple of years later.) The house had to be cleared: many treasured belongings – books, records, letters – got abandoned without a second's thought. Relationships, too.

Our last ever U.K. gig (and first try-out for the Marshalls) was at the LSE. In a frenetic rush – everything seemed to accelerate, like when the weeks of planning have suddenly compressed themselves down to the last few hours before the boat sails. We loaded what was left of our worldly goods into Bessie, played the gig and struck out into the continental unknown. I managed to bust the Selmer PA by accidentally silver-papering a fuse (you can bypass a low-tension fuse by wrapping it with silver paper from a fag packet. You can't do this to a HT fuse, which was the mistake I made); but somehow this didn't seem to matter at the time – suddenly, problems were all in the future, not the past.

I have a copy of a 'profit and loss account and balance sheet' for the Moods, compiled I think by an accountant friend or relative of Bill's, which shows, amongst other things, that we owed Ken Pitt £2,847. We had 2 pounds 11 shillings and 10 pence in the bank.

Italy

The van was home, had been for three days now. Obscure regulations, involving something called a 'customs carnet', meant we couldn't enter France so had to take a long route through Germany. (They say the EU has engendered bureaucracy…) We must have crossed the Channel or the North Sea, on some kind of ferry, to somewhere like Ostend. Then we drove in shifts down through the Low Countries and the Rhine valley and through Switzerland (I recall breakfast in Basle), up and over the Grand St Bernard Pass, winding hairpins up and down to and from the sky, and through the Mont Blanc tunnel. At the top, it was blinding sky blue and snow white when we stopped for a change of driver. Andy produced a joint he'd smuggled across several borders.

At the Swiss-Italian border, at the end of the tunnel, we were stopped by stern Italian frontier police, with guns. We were ordered out of the van, lined up, inspected. Bob was our self-appointed Italian speaker, did know a few words, but he obviously wasn't up to this situation. We were instructed, in gesture language, to open up the back of the van. It wasn't a pleasant sight, even to us: a wall to wall, floor to ceiling amassment of suitcases, bags of unwashed laundry, rotting food remnants;

and behind all that, of course, several hundred pounds' worth of musical equipment, being possibly illegally imported.

The border guards, grim-faced, ordered us to unload the van. We looked around at each other, shrugged and started to haul out the debris. The Italian police let us get on with this for a few minutes, then, unable to stifle their laughter, broke out into huge grins. OK, *va bene, avanti!*, put it all back and get on out of here! *Benvenuti all'Italia!*

I thought then that I was going to like this country.

The van was home. Thirty eight hours on the road, roughly, I calculated, having wound my watch three times. "Fuck Italy", John had said several times as we were packing up after the LSE gig. Now, as we cruised down the Aosta valley on the rollercoaster home slope, through growing fog towards a supposed motorway or autostrada called the A3, somewhere around a place called Torino, which is really Turin, then straight on down to Milan, or Milano, can't miss it man – now, I thought: fuck Italy? Yeah, we just might.

Down the Aosta valley, from that terminal borderpoint hilarity, the icefield and the orange fairground ride of the tunnel, through fog which thickens as we descend, which as you jerk awake snaps your eyes to the windscreen, the filmscreen on which you project the hallucinations or realities of thirty eight hours of no sleep (or was that sleep just now? did I see that in or out of my head?), unsought visuals to the relentless soundtrack of the Transit's machinery, metal and plastic and hydraulics, inanimate awareness grooving with itself in an unending insane organ and percussion jam, the undertow of smells, exhaust leakage, burnt oil, entrapped farts, your own body and breath, down we coast into Italy, whatever that may be…

Via Alfonso Lamarmora, Milano, named after one of

Garibaldi's sidekicks, is bleak. It must be mid-evening, about eight. Dim orange streetlights, shuttered four-storey tenement buildings from the nineteenth century, a few black portico tunnels leading into who knows what dank courtyards behind, cobblestones containing embedded tramlines. It's not quite raining. Bob brakes to a halt.

"I think that's it."

Number 17. A flat-fronted blind-eyed slab of a building. This is meant to be 'Pensione Key', our home for the next eight weeks. We're hobbits arriving at the Prancing Pony. Hearts sink.

"OK, let's just pull over and we can– "

Just then a tram hisses towards us like a fully lit-up ocean liner on speed. Bob manages to lift Bessie up onto the kerb – who knows what would've happened otherwise, no way that tram was stopping. "I'll turn down here, shall I," he suggests, doing so, into the side road which, mercifully, doesn't seem to have any tramlines. We're parked.

There's a moment's stunned inertness, then Roger slides open the nearside door, drops tentative ballet-dancer's legs down the doorwell to Italian soil, or rather tarmac. "Christ, it's fucking freezing!" he states, squinting in like a hopped up rabbit pulling a funny face. We're all craning towards the doorway now, wide awake, except John, who's just stopped quietly snoring and now swears in a muffled kind of way, "I'm staying here," it sounds like.

But he has to move for me to get out, so I lean on him, reach up and gently tap his face and whisper "come on John, wake up, it's time to go to bed."

The front door is huge, twelve feet high, but we notice that there's a kind of sub-door set into it, small enough for a human to creep through. Also that there's a column of buttons, one of them labelled 'Key'. Bob presses it. A voice comes out of a tinny speaker grill: *"Sì?" "Um, siamo il gruppo inglese…"* A buzzer sounds, and the door clicks open. There's an old-fashioned lift, with those sliding iron grills, which we take to the second floor. The door to the right of the lobby is open. A middle-aged lady is waiting there. She's completely unfazed by our appearance, but she doesn't smile – seems a little bit strict. *"Allora, siete arrivati. Vi faccio veder le camere, e poi, avrete fame, ci sono due trattorie, ma quello sul'angolo e chiuso stasera, percio…"* She stops. "I'm sorry. You are English." A smile now. "I forget sometimes. I am Polish, actually. My name is really Kay, but these Italians can't pronounce that properly so I have to call myself Key, K E Y, for them. I show you your rooms – you have four. Follow me."

Quick decisions have to be made, just like the occupation of Hutchings Walk. Graham and I exchange a glance and get to the front of the queue. The first door on the right is ours. It looks fine. Having experienced digs in Blackpool, I'd been expecting something squalid, hoping or wishing for something adequate: this looks luxurious. Two single beds, bedside tables with lamps, stone floor with mats, and a huge wardrobe. (This wardrobe will figure in many of my future dreams and visions, its swirling veneer possessed, at the peak of druggy imagination, by a panopticon of goblins and houris and wraiths…) This was my first experience of the Italian attitude towards habitation – the exterior is irrelevant, you live in the inside of the house. Grim facades can hide marble hallways and delicate antiques. This isn't quite in that class, but it'll do.

We go down to the trattoria which isn't closed (the only time we'll ever eat there, as it turns out: the one on the corner was much better). Nobody, not even Bob, knows how to read the menu, and the waiter has no English, so we all order spaghetti

Bolognese, or some equivalent, and then, because we're still hungry, spaghetti Bolognese again. Going back to the pensione, Andy and I remember something we've forgotten in the van, tell the others to carry on, we'll catch up. When we get back to the front door, it's locked, no reply to the bell; oh well, we think, another night in the van, used to that… Luckily Bob eventually notices we're missing and comes to rescue us. Clean sheets over and under a filthy body have never felt so good.

• • •

Next day, after we'd been allowed to sleep for twelve hours and wash ourselves (Pensione Key had a sumptuous bathroom, with hot water on demand and a deep, wide tub; the soles of my smelly feet were, I noticed, black), we were collected and introduced to our new life. We loaded ourselves into Bessie and followed someone in a car through the centre of Milan, a hardly noticed course which would become, over the coming weeks, a beaten track, a footpath I could follow with my eyes, brain, or sense of balance shut down.

The Piper Club was part of some kind of municipal complex, the Palazzo del'Arte, off the Piazza Castello, on the borders of the Parco Sempione, its status never precisely clear. I'd guess now that this chunk of the Art Palace was leased out by the Commune, the local council, to raise a bit of cash. Certainly, it was controlled by one man, Leo Wachter, my third and greatest nightmare manager.

When we got there, before anything else we were herded into some kind of backroom bar area and instructed by some stressed-out interpreter guy that we had, immediately, to sign a four-page sheaf of blank paper with an official seal at the bottom and top, *carta bollata*. I balked at this: "my mother taught me to never sign a blank sheet of paper!" (Not strictly true, but a good line; quite right mum, but you hadn't encountered Italian bureaucracy then.) It was patiently suggested that if we refused to sign we'd have to go back to England on the next van, whereas if we did these blank sheets were going to become our *'permesso di soggiorno'*, residence permit, pieces of paper permitting our sojourn here – the details above the signatures would of course be filled in later (and then fed into some system and forgotten forever). I briefly huffed and puffed, then signed. There was some hassle about there being only seven of us instead of the eight Arango had seen in the audition (Downes having meanwhile been subtracted and the price therefore reduced), but we didn't argue too much once we realised that each of us still gets the same money, and once we saw the club.

Try as I may, I have no accurate visual memory of the interior of the Piper Club, Milan. That's a great memory! The best places I ever played were empty by daylight, dusty and tawdry at the best, filthy and hazardous at the worst, just spaces waiting to be filled. I think of the Disque, Eel Pie, Swanage drill hall, even the Cromwellian. None of that matters. In fact, if anyone even notices it, it's failed, because this is not a restaurant. You don't go there to admire the décor or sample the canapés – you go to fill the space with noise and people. And this space was waiting to be filled.

The stage was the biggest and best we'd ever had. Wide, so we could spread out, not too deep, so the sound wouldn't get lost in caverns behind us (how many times had we suffered from that acoustic nightmare), just the right height that the girls and boys couldn't quite reach up and grab us, but thought it worth a try. Enough room to set up these brand-new Marshall stacks, crank them up to eleven, experiment with sound results… My nagging concern about the silver-papered Selmer PA I'd killed back there centuries ago at the LSE dissolved away once we saw the Semprini house installation: six two metre tall column speakers on stands around the hall, fed by about six hundred watts through a mixing desk we weren't allowed to touch, from about as many mic inputs as we could provide (three at the time, though we later got a couple more Shures, one paid for by me out of my wages, where is it?).

We set up and played a couple of numbers. I struggled with the Marshall, wasn't used to controlling that much power, also finding it hard to get the sound I needed for my Telecaster Steve Cropper licks through an amp designed for Clapton/Hendrix overdrive power fuzz. I probably should have kept the Fender. But that small box, usually perched on a borrowed chair, would not have suited at all in Milan, Italy. The point about managing expectations is to set it up so that they hardly exist (the kids of Milan had no idea what was about to hit them) and then confound them. We needed to be big, unexpected, intimidating and a bit nasty. Marshall stacks were a good starter. And of course I wanted to play Clapton/Hendrix overdrive power fuzz, amongst many other things.

Next day, we met Leo Wachter for the first time, in his office. He looked like Joe Stalin, the heavy features, the thick moustache overflowing his mouth, the body language. He spoke no English, delivering his welcome address via an interpreter, the same guy who'd made us sign the forms the day before. I don't remember the content of this speech (it was definitely a speech, no space for questions or conversation), but the gist was clear. We play, he pays. Lines of communication were drawn: any problems, talk to so-and-so, or another such-and-such, Leo always available in case of issues… damn good management-speak. You had to respect the guy (he made that quite clear) but at the same time you couldn't help liking him and his charm (he did that well too). We left the office fairly elated, ate something somewhere, went back to Pensione Key and slept for another twelve hours. First gig was the next night.

Once again, I found myself surfing on the crest of no expectations. Back in England, I'd assumed that I was going to some primitive world, where the people would be ignorant peasants or arrogant waiters, where guitar strings and plectrums would be an exotic import, where music itself, at least our sort, would be an obscure, exotic import from a foreign, colonising land. I'd stocked up on strings and plecs in London on this ignorant assumption.

It wasn't like that. The first night at the Piper, the first time we played live to a heaving audience, in our shiny new coats and shirts, I got back that feeling I'd had the first time I stepped up onto the stage at the Wheelhouse, never before performing in public but suddenly realising the power you control when you're up there, knowing that whatever you do, however mad or incompetent, will jerk their behaviour just where and how you want. Play James Brown's *I Go Crazy* and they'll sway side to side. Play *Shout* and they'll jump up and down. Play *Loving You Too Long*, they'll smooch and snog.

Now, I'm amazed by how my innate timidity vanishes when I get to perform in public. At a party, even today, I'll be reluctant to take the initiative in conversations, I'll hover in the background waiting for somebody to come and kick-start me – I'm not any kind of extrovert initiator. But put me on a stage, of any kind, where I'm in control… and that was some stage, the Piper Milan.

We only had to do an hour, one set, at nine. Later on, the start time might get shifted, according to the attendance. This was fine by us, we preferred playing to that mob of pressurised teenage Italian hormones, male or female, it got us going too. Over a few nights, we discovered a few bars, the Mexico is one I remember, and a restaurant in Piazza Cordusio, just a short hop from the Piper on the way home, the Rosengarten, which seemed happy to stay open as long as a customer survived and could order another drink, a Forst beer in a *stecca*, a boot-shaped glass which you had to drink the right way round or else the beer would go down your shirt rather than your neck – try it sometime, if you are, or want to be, German. It being February, only the indoor part was accessible; it'd be a while before we uncovered the outside canopied courtyard, tables and chairs under vines or clematis rampaging over some kind of wood pergola in the late night summer heat...

On stage, I was back at the Swanage Drill Hall, up there on a good platform, deploying hot guitar skills, lots of pretty nice little girls jumping around down in the pit. Incredible that the same crowd would turn up every night of the week to hear us play exactly the same set, the already stale one we'd brought with us from England; we certainly didn't have the time or inclination to work up new material, even if there'd been any available. This didn't matter too much. For the first time we had steady work and income. It actually tightened us back up as a music machine, it was like a continual rehearsal. The pressures and hassle of travelling, finding food and accommodation, setting up and sussing out the venue, dismantling the kit, repacking the van and getting back on the road, with the actual performance an almost irrelevant distraction in between – all that had been magically taken away. All we had to do was turn up and play.

And we did. By the end of the Piper gig, we were probably tighter musically than ever (although the music itself wasn't quite as good as it had been in the Dave Anthony/Pete Sweet days). We started to get real stage presence too, unashamedly playing up or down to an adoring audience, screaming girls and tempo-nodding boys, our own little Beatlemania moment. I discovered a few stagecraft tricks, picking out and eye-contacting just one girl, smiling or winking or making appropriate gestures with the nut end of my guitar.

• • •

And then there was the culture shock, surprise, amazement. It was a bit like Leeds, except for the content. A new language, bewilderingly different food, alien architecture and street rules and social expectations, it was devastatingly exciting. I decided I had to learn a bit of the language, or how was I going to communicate with those girls? So I got a book and sussed out the grammar, learnt as many verbs as I could (especially the irregular ones, which proved remarkably parallel to English – be, do, have, etc – they don't have 'get'). The nouns could come later, once you'd put the structures together. *'Come si chiama...?'* was a useful phrase ('what's that called?', or in the charming literal translation 'how does that call itself?'). I reckon I was once again applying the learning process I'd taken out of my university career – focus, gather, analyse – just like I'd done in the glassworks office but with much more confidence and concentration. I took Italian on board pretty fast, a speed curve comparable to my guitar-chord take-on back at the birth of the skiffle days in 1956.

Our name was deemed to be a problem. I didn't entirely agree – the sophisticated Milanese youth mostly spoke or at least understood a bit of English, and had mastered the 'th' sound, which doesn't exist in spoken Italian and so is quite alien to the phonetic orthography of the language. The 'y' at the end of 'Anthony' didn't present an issue: 'i' is called 'e' in the Italian alphabet, so 'y', which sounds exactly the same, becomes 'e lunga', 'long i'. But the 'th' in 'Anthony', which had to be pronounced 't', was possibly asking a bit too much. Quite reasonably, we were asked if we'd object to being billed, on posters and suchlike, as 'Dave Antony's Moods'. (Funnily enough, the early Kenneth Pitt publicity shot I showed you previously contains this version of the name, that time as a spelling mistake.) As the name itself really didn't mean a thing by now (I'm not sure why we retained it, we could have been just 'The Moods'; possibly it was thought that we'd get confused with the Moody Blues), and Dave himself wasn't around to protest, we went along without a murmur. I think I wanted to rename the band 'Water' or something by this stage.

The food took a bit longer to get into. We had to eat every day, but what to eat was another question. Cooking up our own corned beef hash wasn't an option anymore. It was about reading, understanding and ordering from menus – and no-one knew anything about foreign food. This is where the nouns start to come in. Bill, spotting the word *'inglese'*, English, in *'fegato al'inglese'*, asked me as the least worst Italian speaker what *'fegato'* was. I didn't have a clue, bluffed, said "not sure, but nice", turned out he hated liver. Just because it was the most expensive item on the Rosengarten menu, 1300 lire, I ordered *'filetto alla tartara'*. The English-speaking waiter frowned and caught my eye: "are you sure? *Carne cruda?*". It was too late to back down. So a plate full of raw minced steak, raw egg, and a whole pile of unidentifiable raw vegetables and pickles turned up and got professionally churned into what became, actually, a seriously delicious plateful of, well, raw mince. I don't think I ordered it a second time. But it scored me a few points at the time: it does no harm to your status to have your colleagues gawp at you whilst you do something awesome.

In Milan, I had to find my way around, just like after Leeds or London, but foreign. My geographic sense is good but slow. I need my own time to learn a place. In the case of Leeds and London I hadn't really been granted that time, because there'd always been somewhere I had to be before I'd learnt the way. Milan was different, seemed slower. During the day, if you were up and running (around midday we'd get gently turfed out of our beds by Anna, the cleaning lady), you could spend the afternoon drifting around the city centre, accidentally coming across the Galleria Vittorio Emanuele II and some other *gallerie*, arcades; the Duomo, Lawrence's massive yet diaphanous gothic hedgehog; the seedy intriguing Brera district just down behind the Rosengarten, useful shops near the Pensione Key, and dark blind alleys off the via Dante. I stumbled over La Scala (closed for refurbishment). And Messagerie Musicale, where you could get every kind of guitar strings, plectrums and rare expensive US import albums.

By about week five, I was just starting to feel this city, see my way through yet another cloud of fog. I lost my way once, late at night, drunk, and couldn't ask directions of a policeman because I couldn't say where I wanted to go. I couldn't remember the name of the road I lived in. Via Lamafromoa or something. He couldn't really help but had nothing to arrest me for; I think I said 'Duomo', got pointed towards the Hedgehog, nearly got mugged in via Dante by a couple of Milanese thugs but somehow Englished my way out, an early acquired, often deployed skill which consisted of shrugging and deferentially hand-spreading and saying *'non capisco, sono inglese'*, which usually got you away from that kind of stuff. (Italian has an even richer range of descriptors than English for this sort of person: *sciemo, idiota, stronzo, ebete, deficiente, testa di cazzo, pirla…*)

• • •

Sometime towards the end of this eight week Piper gig, we were called in to Leo's office. To nobody's surprise, we were offered an open-ended extension. Leo would buy out Pitt's contract and employ us as a salaried item in his growing Larry Parnes-style stable of English and Italian acts. He would also finance a two week holiday back in the U.K., by air! There were all sorts of other components to the offer. It couldn't be refused. In fact it wasn't even discussed. Mine would have been the only dissenting voice, if I'd thought about it for a few minutes; but

I didn't do that, at least not properly. If I had, the band would have carried on without me, and probably gone the same way it eventually did, and I would have ended up somewhere else unknown. Instead I floated on the current, again.

It was the third time I'd been on an aeroplane. The first two had been rickety prop-driven hops from Eastleigh to Jersey and back, when I was nine or ten, for some long-forgotten holiday with my aunt, on my own. Why did my parents subject me to that? I can't imagine I asked for it; perhaps I had to be got out of the way for a few days, there was certainly some dark mysterious family stuff going on at that time. I do remember getting off the plane at Eastleigh on my return. You had to get your suitcase and park it on a trestle table in customs, and wait until a uniform came to you and chalked a rune on the case and indicated you were free to go. All this had been kind of explained to me in advance, but no-one had thought to instruct me about what to do if it went wrong in any way. As it was, I got totally overlooked and ended up standing there on my own in front of the bench with my sad little ten-year-old's unchalked suitcase, all the uniforms having disappeared, until at last my father stopped hovering outside, noticed that I was missing, poked his head round the screen, plucked up his courage and rescued me.

This 1967 flight wasn't a bit like that. The plane may have been a de Havilland Comet 4, I can't be sure, but it was a swish jetliner, no question. We felt important. Not many ordinary people got to fly in those days, never mind on Comets. The Alps were a black and white 3-D movie from above, the black deep granite valleys (a hint of dark green down below the snowline), the white snow on the tops, sometimes shading down into glacial blue or ice-grey... and here we are up here, viewing this film, cosseted in our comfy cinema seats and being attentively looked after by nice girls in smart uniforms.

In England, the summer of love was about to begin, but there were no signs of that round my way. My brother picked me up from Heathrow and carted me back to Bournemouth. I looked around. Details had of course changed. La Fiesta was long dead, and the kids had long moved on. The Disque had vanished, so had the Wheelhouse, and the Badger was a sad, empty hole. El Cabala was still just about alive, but the juke-box had gone. I went down there and somehow contrived an awkward split with a leftover girlfriend, clearing the decks. She said "I can wait for you", but I hadn't previously noticed her halitosis. I couldn't wait to get back to Italy.

So we went back. The rooms at Pensione Key (or 'Mama's' as we'd come to know it by then, Roger having christened Signora Kay thus a week or two after we arrived, to her hospitable amusement) had been held, warmly welcoming. Leo had lined up some big gigs. The day after our return there was a huge stadium concert in Milan (possibly San Siro), we being one act among many from the Leo Wachter stable. We had short residencies at the other Piper Clubs in Rome and Torino. Once, we played warm-up support to no less than Sammy Davis Jnr at a big concert hall in Rome. I shook hands with him as he went on: he said something like "nice, man", but I've no idea whether he'd actually heard us. (I count it as a good review anyway – and I shook hands with Sammy Davis Jnr!)

The Milan Piper should obviously have been played out, but that didn't seem to stop us going back there, over and over. I have an enduring memory of hearing Sergeant Pepper for the first time in the backstage band room there, on a tape acquired somehow by Maurizio, the leader of the top Italian group of the time, the Equipe 84. This must have been early June, just as the record came out. Obviously, my love affair with the squiggly groove burst into flames again, and this time I felt in a position to do something about it.

The Burgess sessions at Abbey Road had been frustrating. I could see what was going on, mic placements, equalisation, screening and so on, and I wanted to control it even though I hadn't a clue how. Pepper, and others which followed, opened my ears and mind (both boosted by copious amounts of hash) to the potential of the studio as more than just a frozen live gig, as a musical instrument in its own right, a hidden extra band member. Soon after our return, I started to agitate towards the need for us to make a record – not an issue actually, nobody disagreed. Also, it turned out that Leo, or another of his tentacles, controlled a record company called SAAR, with a studio somewhere in the northern outskirts of Milan.

That group, Equipe 84, was to have a powerful influence on our subsequent career. I have been told (and Wikipedia seems to concur) that there was a mystique about their name at the time, some obscure numerology thing. If I'd heard that then, I would undoubtedly have scuttered down that road, because I was starting to swerve into the soft verges of the mystic. I was reading Pynchon and R D Laing. My recollection, though, is that they named themselves after a bottle of Italian brandy, Stock 84.

We got pretty friendly during the next few months. Roger was particularly matey with the drummer, Alfio, in a dangerously edgy way – they shared a girlfriend, Inez, and no-one knew whether this was consensual or not. I had analytical debates with Maurizio, on the pavement outside the Piper, about whether the solo on Penny Lane was a piccolo trumpet or a speeded-up ordinary trumpet (I was right – look it up). They made what seemed to me to be state of the art records. *29 Settembre*, their current hit, was a multi-layered guitar based production, sonically drawing on the Byrds and Buffalo Springfield, an intriguing story-song which seemed to come out of my Leeds-learnt existentialist background, time twists and ambiguities, by a young writer called Lucio Battisti.......

. . .

Our big number at the time was *My Baby*, a song I'd picked up in one of my London record shop haunts in about October 66, written by Jerry Ragovoy and Mort Shuman, and recorded by Garnett Mimms. I loved this record, because of its subtle shifts between three and four beat bars, the stop time release (it all slows down) where you're fooled into thinking it's over until the tension gets released as it kicks back into the three-four, the brass-led punchiness of the arrangement. Roger loved it too, as a singer's song, as you'll hear if you listen to it. The Italian crowds seemed to like it when we did it live. It was a shoo-in for our first Italian single. So we went in to SAAR studio, producer-less.

The end product was less than perfect. Listening to it now, its defects outweigh its merits as a record. The whole sound is muddy. The brass is practically inaudible (compare this sound to *Give It a Chance* a year previously). Roger's great performance is spoilt by over-recording, into red distortion. The overall performance is plodding, no fire: we'd been doing it live for six months, and it shows – we were bored with the song by the time we got it into the studio. It's a bit of a mess, actually. The brass intro's nice though. Had *Try a Little Tenderness* come out by then? If not, this is an uncanny premonition. I think we mixed the horn track back through my newly acquired wah-wah pedal. (This was a promotional gift, presumably from Vox's Italian reps via Leo. I had no idea how to play with this toy, until a bit later I heard *Axis Bold As Love* and *Disraeli Gears*).

But the heat was on, and this had to be it. So we needed a B side. I'd been writing proper songs for about two years by now, mostly derivative, mostly totally un-Moods; and back in 66, in Hutchings Walk, I'd started to construct one, *Fading Away*, that seemed to be a cross between *Good Vibrations* and *Reach Out (I'll be There)*. In this case, the chords were everything. I'm not sure how conscious this was, but I felt that I had here a possible crossover between several of the shifting swirling elements of music as it was then – black soul, west coast romanticism, incipient psychedelia: I wanted it all.

It's not the best record we made (that has to be *New Directions*), but it might be the most interesting. Even today, despite its obvious flaws, it gives me a buzz. Roger hated the song, got some of the words wrong, but nevertheless gave it enough. Graham's trombone solo in the Wilson-like bridge is stilted; given more time he could have made it more legato, slipped in a bit of vibrato. The whole thing is much too fast. The coda should have been even more daring. (If we'd ever played it live, I can imagine a ten minute freak-out.)

The lyrics are, I think, quite good. It starts ambiguously, as if the singer is commiserating with his friend about a break-up – 'I know just how it feels' – and continues in this vein, graphically describing that feeling, 'hazy grey like a winter sky', 'your eyes see only an empty room'. Then, suddenly, as the music changes, the shouted punchline: 'because of me!' So you wonder for a moment: is he apologising to his friend – has he nicked his girl? But in the second verse, you realise that he's not addressing a friend, he's actually apologising to the girl for their break-up, whilst rationalising and defending his behaviour, pretending that they can put it all behind them and he can wriggle out – 'what can I do when the love that's still in you has gone from me?'. In the middle bit, he confesses that he had, in fact, loved her, and this emotional breakdown is reflected in the sad instrumental passage (I originally wrote some words for this, then realised that they weren't needed). In the end, the singer ducks and weaves out – 'just like everything… there's nothing anybody can do'. All in all, an interesting record. It crops up occasionally on obscure bootleg compilations (one review, perplexingly, compares it to Simon Dupree and the Big Sound).

The Joker Records label credits the song to 'Tim Walker – Wavan'. Obviously, I'm Tim Walker. I was embarrassed by my real surname: this stems from ribbing at prep school. (I looked it up. The surname 'Large' in fact derives from the identically spelt French word meaning 'generous', as in 'largesse'. This made me feel better: but I don't have the courage to pronounce it with the soft French G. Yet. I also recently realised that it's an anagram of 'Elgar'). Wavan – and this is why this is important – was Leo Wachter's musical frontman, a guy called Valerio Vancheri. I don't know if this person exists, or whether he ever composed a note of music, but I do know that he had nothing at all to do with the composition of *Fading Away*. This was the first hint that Leo was stealing from us, directly.

At every gig, we were supposed to fill in a sort of 'performing rights' form listing the numbers we'd played, so that royalties would be justly distributed to the authors of the songs (I think a similar system existed in England, and was similarly ignored). The first ten or so slots were always pre-filled with Italian titles we couldn't even translate, never mind play, but all apparently composed by this Wavan and his collaborators. Of course, we just stuck in a few more items, with famous composers such as Adolf Hitler, Harold Wilson or Beatrix Potter, or Fred Splonge, signed the form and forgot it. It was a joke, in fact I seem to remember some degree of competition in coming up with the most outrageous titles and writers. That was just a laugh, and didn't affect us directly in any way. But when Wavan appeared as a composer credit for *Fading Away*, that was a bit different. That was direct theft, from me. If Signor Vancheri exists and would like to get in touch, I'd be happy to accept my share of those stolen royalties.

• • •

Chronology gets confused here. It's a single event, a three-month one-off event. I can remember it, I was there, no doubt about that; but piecing it all back together, like some kind of history or consecutive film, well, the summer of 1967 just didn't work that way. It was one huge single event, within which passage of time, logical cause and effect, were incidental. The drugs helped. In a dope-induced eternal present, before, after, back then and what if next are not operands: now is all that counts. My memories are conditioned by that. But this is meant to be some kind of history, which requires chronology, so here goes. I'm going to be quoting from my demented diaries of the time, without attribution. Spot me if you can.

Towards the spring, the big break came along. Leo announced that he had booked us as support act on a tour of Italy by The New Vaudeville Band.

> DOMENICA 9 LUGLIO - Ore 21,15
> **STADIO COMUNALE BENTEGODI**
> Piazzale Olimpia - VERONA
>
> eccezionale spettacolo musicale
> ANNA MASCOLO della RAI-TV presenta
>
> **SUPER PIPER'S SHOW n. 3**
>
> con la favolosa The New Vaudeville Band e con The Dave Antony's Moods, The Bad Boys, Ombretta Colli e il suo complesso, The Honey Beats, Umberto e il suo complesso, Igor Mann e i Gormanni, The Holls, Balletto The Kitten di Franco Estill.
>
> PREZZI POLTRONE L. 1.000 - GRADINATE L. 500
>
> I biglietti sono in vendita presso: Cit, Caffè Massaua, Toresela Piper's, Bar Zanatta, Autogrill, Azienda Soggiorno Boscochiesanuova.
> Lo spettacolo è ideato dal'organizzazione Marco Neddoli

This wholly manufactured band, put together to cash in on the chart success of *Winchester Cathedral*, a delightful dandelion clock of whimsy the previous year, were evidently still viable enough, perhaps riding just behind the crest of the wave of English retro-psychedelia the Beatles had pioneered on Revolver and consolidated on Pepper, closely followed by the Small Faces, the Move and countless others. (Even the Cream had succumbed, with *Wrapping Paper*.) This curious sub-genre was rooted in syncopated four/four rhythms, augmented and diminished chords, inscrutably romantic lyrics, and, often, corny horn parts. Andy loved it, harking back as it did to his roots in 1930s novelty big bands, Cab Calloway and, indeed, Andy's namesake, and we were all sympathetic to this style. One of our live features was an a capella performance, led by Andy straight out of this tradition, of *Down By The Riverside*, complete with coon-show open-palmed hand gestures. (I have an almost certainly unplayable acetate of a drug- booze-fuelled studio version of this.)

I'd even written several songs in this vein, none of which, mercifully, have ever made it to tape. So it wasn't quite such a crappy gig as it might now appear – indeed, no conceivable gig would have seemed crappy: we were desperate to get playing again, would have toured with The Laughing Policeman had he been working. Also, the tour contained a troupe of five rather enticing girl dancers, the Kittens. I subsequently learnt that these girls had made a bet amongst themselves that each of them would go to bed with each of us. This was a giggly girly fantasy on both sides. Of the five, I fancied two. Of the two, one was a sixteen year old virgin who thought a quick snog on the bus would cover her bet; the other was a slinky redhead with whom I'd have gladly done a deal, except that she went down with measles half way through the tour.

Also half way through the tour, it became obvious that money was being lost. Italy hadn't, after all, fallen in love with the New Vaudeville Band. We were playing to embarrassingly empty venues. After a week of this, we were told without notice that Leo's promise to pay all our expenses, on top of our salaries, was revoked – so we were suddenly much poorer than we'd become accustomed to. There was no explanation – one day the bills were being paid, the next the whole company had to pay their own. None of this lined up with our expectations. I think this is fair comment: once again we became the victims of inadequate management, this time of someone who saw musicians as an exploitable resource rather than an artistic asset, whose sole motivation was personal profit, and most importantly who knew sod-all about actual music and, when his commercial judgement turned out to be even worse than his musical, viciously turned upon and penalised his artists. Discontent reached a high level on that tour. Leo eventually managed to smooth things over, with the tremendous charm he could muster when he chose to, but the damage was done, and the restless ambitious minds started to wander.

The tour itself, of course, mostly visiting small cities or towns in the north or centre of the country, was an eye-opening experience. Although we'd been, by now, to big places like Turin and Rome as well as Milan, this was really the first close-up experience of the real Italy. We now had a road manager called Franco, of whom we were a bit scared because his face had been horribly scarred by a fire a year or so earlier. Franco was actually one of the most charming men I've ever known, and possessed an impish sense of humour of a kind not all Italians have. Once, in a big car park outside some venue, after the van had been unloaded, he attached a speaker cable to Bessie's front bumper, put her in first gear, then got out and led her across the car park like a huge, docile blue sheepdog. Come to think of it, Franco probably suffered from a certain degree of secondary smoking.

Anyway, being relieved of much of the physical onus made me, at least, feel freer to explore. Once the venue had been located, equipment unloaded and set up, hotel found and rooms negotiated, there were usually a few hours when you could just go out and wander. You could cross wide empty market squares, wondering why the local people always walk round the sides, never across the middle; poke into porticos and peer through the windows of closed shops with names like 'Macellaio', 'Parucchiere', 'Drogheria' (this one looked promising, we'd learnt the word for 'drugs', but it turned out to be a grocer's), examine the architecture and absorb the details of what letterboxes and phone booths looked like, what street signs and advertising posters meant, and how it was that certain shops seemed to be officially licensed to sell tobacco and salt. I learnt the country this way.

Apparently, one of the other bands in this package was an English group called the Bad Boys, with a keyboard player called Chris Dennis. I don't remember them at all.

In May, we went back into the studio with a producer called David Pardoe, who'd been shipped in as a response to my demands. We needed another record. One night, in via Lamarmora, John mentioned that he'd heard this record on the radio, which sounded a bit like *When a Man Loves a Woman*. Of course, it was *A Whiter Shade of Pale*.

Next day we advised Pardoe that we wanted this song. We felt ourselves to be in a position to make this kind of demand. A few days later, he came back with a set of Italian lyrics, which Roger was intensively coached in. Soon after that, we went into the SAAR studio. I think the whole of the first session was spent with me and Bob going through the organ part, decomposing the counterpoint and the drawbar shifts and the Leslie whooshes – possibly our best musical collaboration. He loved it, of course. The rest of the band mostly sat around, wondering what their job would be. At some point, Andy suggested doubling parts of the top Hammond line on trumpet and trombone, not in any upfront way but as a delicate, muted reinforcement, an almost unnoticeable little lift. The SAAR engineers' inability to record brass properly actually played in our favour for once – a punchy Memphis Horns or Funk Brothers treatment would have been fatal.

A few days later, an embarrassed David Pardoe informed us that we'd been hijacked. A rival set of Italian lyrics had surfaced and been sold to a native band called, charmingly, the Dik Dik. We were pretty pissed off, of course – ripped off and lied to once more – but we went ahead and re-recorded the vocal in English. Roger was naturally more comfortable and gave it his best.

The lying Pardoe reported that Denny Cordell, the producer of the Procol Harum original, had heard our version and found it better than theirs. I briefly swallowed this then discounted it –

I think some feedback came from England to the effect of 'must be joking'. Actually, liar or not, Pardoe was right. I've just listened to the two versions, side by side. Try the experiment. Ours is superior in every respect – recording quality, arrangement, performance. Apart from the trivial point that we hadn't written the song, and stood no chance of nicking the Italy hit from the pre-purchased Dik Dik.

Once again, we needed a B side. By now, my songwriting had spun off in many opposite directions. I was pastiching all over the place, mostly Dylan – we'd missed out on two Dylan hits, I wasn't about to present another. Pardoe came up with a demo of a song called *Talking to the Rain*, which we quite liked. We went into the studio, I did my usual souping-up of the arrangement, and we knocked it off in an afternoon. It's pretty slick and very catchy, though once again let down by incompetent recording and bad balance. I have no emotional attachment at all to it. That turned out to be our last officially released recording.

...

In the summer of 67 we had a two week residency at l'Altro Mondo, Riccione, on the Adriatic just down from Rimini. The Other World. This was unlike any venue we'd played before. From the outside it looked like a warehouse. I've spoken before about the anonymity of locales, how the atmosphere is created from what goes on, not what it goes on in. Well, when you got in, l'Altro Mondo turned that on its head. Even empty, by daylight, this was obvious. The stainless steel central dance floor; the scaffolding-supported split level wall-less rooms in which you could dance, drink, just sit, or do who knows what else; the huge lighting gantries, the import of which we could only guess the first time we walked in there to set up. It was more than just an empty room waiting to be filled: it was a space challenging you to fill it. I quote from my sparse diary of the time: '… a fabulous club, probably the best we've ever played in – the lighting fantastic, and the crowds during this holiday period were knowledgeable and highly appreciative. It all brought out the best in us, we'd never performed so well.'

Some time before this, we'd managed to source some pot from a couple of guys, the vestiges of a West Indian steel band, marooned in Milan due to mysterious visa-related problems and seemingly indefinitely resident in the pensione across the landing from Key's (Signora Scotti), with obviously good contacts and no particular need to play music for a living. At any rate, I never saw a steel drum. One of them was called Carlo, I forget the other guy's name though he was the one who actually got us the dope. Carlo was an aspiring writer, of short stories, so we related a bit. I remember one story, four pages long, the punchline of which was that the whole plot had unravelled within the confines of the schematic map of the London Underground. Maybe Carlo inadvertently invented Mornington Crescent?

So we were primed and ready for l'Altro Mondo. Leo booked us into a small pensione on the inland outskirts of Riccione, in the dusty summer countryside. There were plastic tables and chairs on the terrace, where you could eat your stuffed tomatoes and grilled chicken (the latter delivered mid-morning, not yet grilled, in fact still squawking, by an old man on a moped). In the afternoon, we shipped down to Riccione beach, purloined loungers and slept on them, waking up for the occasional swim. Years later I wrote a song, called *Italian Jobs*, about this and other adventures: here are the first lines, from memory: 'The Princess of Parma belly-flops from her yacht into the Adriatic sea with an aristocratic splash; while the young Valentino on the cabin roof is sipping his Bacardi and browsing his Balzac paperback...' I was observing, you see: this was a scene I was on the fringe of, tantalisingly close to – but unable to make that final jump into the pool of swimming or drowning engagement. As usual, I stood back. Another line: '... and then Trader John says there's a *festa* at Cattolica and somebody told me that somebody sold them...' But I didn't go to the *festa* at Cattolica. Andy did, and came back laden with drugs, in his pockets and himself.

We lay on the beach, soaked up the sun, and heard our *Whiter Shade of Pale* being broadcast through loudspeakers all along the seafront. A rare photograph in my memory – the sun and pale rippling Adriatic, the white hotels behind, and a swell of emotion like a tickle of breeze across the body-packed beach, girls suddenly looking up from their sunbeds and smiling as this elusive sound phases out of the distant tinny speakers, like Ambre Solaire onto their brown bikini-strapped backs. And that surge of feeling soaking into my backbone.

Two days before the end of the two week gig, Bill was rushed into hospital. This was real appendicitis, not the sort we'd made John fake seven months before at the Brixton Ram Jam. They operated the next morning. Against our will, we did a short spot without bass, but it was pretty atrocious.

When he was sufficiently recovered, Bill expressed the wish to go to England for his convalescence. Leo agreed and, as we understood it, offered to pay the plane fare and advance some money for Bill to live on in the meantime. Pardoe arrived from Sicily. Leo was naturally enough unhappy at losing money because we couldn't work – I seem to remember a debate about how was it that we couldn't function without a bass player, which we won – but he must have been mollified by our assurances that we could usefully spend the time in the studio, me or John playing bass on the records. We wanted our Pepper (or at least I wanted mine) and Leo, the businessman, must've noticed that albums were where it was at; the Beatles, after all, had dug their heels in and refused to play live any more, on the stated grounds that the technology wasn't up to reproducing their recorded sound on stage, but actually because it was much more fun to piss around in the studio, a rationalisation I think every member of the Moods, and David Pardoe, was comfortable with.

So, over that summer, we went into SAAR a few more times. I wanted an album, like *Pepper* or *Piper at the Gates of Dawn* (which my brother had smuggled over on a holiday visit with my parents – I have several sub-Syd songs in my archives). I had a pretty little song called *Jennifer Browne*, out of *She's Leaving Home*, which we record d twice. Roger wrote a ballad called *So Nice*, which has recently surfaced from the internet. There was a weird, totally atypical drug-crazed thing called *See My Soul* (now available on a compilation called Rare Mod Vol 2', AJX

226), jammed with double tracking, backwards cymbals, and what was meant to be some kind of oriental modal nose flute riff or something, which Bob obstinately pretended to be unable to play (because he hated it – I slightly regret my frustrated outburst 'calls himself a fucking musician?' – but not that much, a fucking musician would've played the fucking notes, like them or not, wouldn't he.)

My personal influences were infiltrating the band, the antithesis of where we'd started. They all went along with me, of course, I'd become the default leader. I had no idea of this at the time. I had no idea that I was the strongest personality amongst this lot – and so, I suppose now, I must have seen their deference as resistance, perhaps lightly salted with resentment. I once had a fight with Roger – he actually hit me in the face, not very hard but it scared me – and when we talked afterwards, and I asked him "why?", he said "maybe I'm a bit scared of you". I still don't understand that.

We were wasting time. In 1967, after Pepper, the Beatles were given the freedom of Abbey Road, and spent bucket-loads of EMI money sitting in Studio 2 trying to write and record, money flushed down the drain of failed creativity, resulting in the mostly vacuous outcome of *Magical Mystery Tour*. I put us into that same pathetic path. The path was clear and shining – everybody can do anything, and you and your self-belief are all it needs. But in their case, they were at least diverging or decaying from an original core of solid communal creativity: in ours, there'd never been any kind of core, once Pete and Dave had gone. This didn't dilute the arrogance one bit: I distinctly remember once telling Leo, or one of his minions, that Pardoe was not for us and we wanted George Martin, if you'd be so kind. I cringe even now to recall the smiling acquiescence with which this ludicrous demand was met, to imagine what they must have been thinking behind the smiles and nods.

Bill came back, after some persuasion (the apron strings possibly still not quite unknotted), but we didn't get back to work. We were stuck in Milan. Milan in August is a stinking dusty sweltering ghost town. The shops and bars have pulled their shutters down, the taxi drivers, those who are left, have wilted and crawled off to their balconies, the waiters in the few remaining *trattorie* sit and snooze in back, dreading the entrance of a customer. The dogshit has dried into crusts on the pavements. You can walk around the city centre all day and encounter ten people. I loved it.

Actually, we shouldn't have been there, indolent, pissing about in recording studios. We should have been out on the sweaty road, bashing it out in hot clubs or cool open air fiestas, honing our craft. But we didn't think we wanted that, and Leo convinced himself that he didn't want that either. He had this perverted idea, beloved of impresarios the world over, that assets had to be held back, conserved till his strategy told him it was time to release them on the world. He was built in the mould of all megalomaniacs, and with all the same behaviours – I think I've already drawn the parallel with Joe Stalin, and it's spot on (except that he didn't actually murder us).

• • •

Roger had, as I've said, been getting pretty close to the Equipe 84, especially the drummer Alfio. Secret discussions were held during the Riccione gig. Roger preferred intrigue and convolution to any form of straightforward dealings with other people. In a small community, whoever first assumes this approach gains power, and this power manifests itself as paranoia. So to some degree the band was losing its integrity. The sleeping arrangements at Via Lamarmora may have encouraged this inclination towards mini-cliques: Bill and Roger; me and Graham; and a reluctant ménage of Bob, John and Andy. I had no reason whatsoever to believe that those other rooms were conspiring, for or against, or just excluding me: which of course served only to fuel the insecurity, you can only be paranoid if you're not sure, can't you?

The drugs probably didn't help much either, though Graham and I used them mostly for listening to music on my little record player. One summer afternoon up at SAAR studios, we'd nipped out the back for a quick puff and found a huge pile of dumped LPs, without sleeves, obviously quality-control rejects. Most of them were crap, but there were some Atlantic jazz items – I forget the details, but let's say Mingus, early Coltrane, Ornette Coleman – which we stole and smoked out until the early hours. I mentioned earlier one of Graham's profundities from this time, but here's another, after a time-stretching session of, probably, 'Free Jazz': he looked across at me and said "why do they play like that?" For my part, I brought in *Smiley Smile* and the Ronettes' first album. It was a bit like those Southbourne days of musical confusion.

Was there a conspiracy going on, and if so, behind whose backs? When it came to the crunch, everyone whizzed off in their own different direction. Roger recruited me as his fall guy, somehow ensuring that when the showdown came, I'd be up at the front while he and the others lowered their faces behind me. Leo did good eye contact. I was never personally involved in the discussions – I can't call them negotiations – with the Equipe 84. Roger and Alfio cooked the whole deal up, possibly with some connivance from others. Dischi Ricordi were solidly behind us. We would just walk away from the version of the Pitt contract which Leo had bought, and be free to start all over, free of financial and professional obligations. Easy.

There was some betrayal involved in there, because one late summer night we were sitting round a table at the Rosengarten when Leo suddenly stormed in, and a couple of involved girls faded off like zephyrs. I can't remember their names or faces, but I'd like to confront them today – I'm sure I'd spit before they did. Leo sat down, did his big avuncular smile, and told us – me – we were free to go. All we had to do was repay him what we owed him, a calculation which he proceeded to jot down on the back of a menu. It was a blinding amount of money, about 25 million lire, and very detailed, down to the last meal and shirt. As he wrote, I could see that he'd done his homework, but he was throwing in everything he could come up with, stuff it had never been suggested constituted any kind of loan or debt. I was shocked and angry, above all about the way I'd been set up. But at that moment, I'm a bit proud to recall, I near enough kept my cool. With hindsight, I should have somehow distracted him and just snatched that menu and stuffed it in my inside pocket – what would he have done then, I wonder, attacked me physically? And would the others have come to my rescue? Instead I smiled and said "OK, I understand. Can I have this?"

The menu vanished into Leo's own pocket. "Oh no."

Actually, of course, with another injection of hindsight, we should have denied everything. Our plans weren't in place, they were just aspirations. Certainly no obligations had been written down. You'd have thought we'd have learnt by now, that we were the ones with the power, because we made the music. The Leos, Pitts, Gunnells could not survive for a week without us and our like, whereas kill all of them and we'd still be functioning. The Alfios and Dischi Ricordi might have seemed to offer a way out, but how were they to be trusted either?

So, that evening at the Rosengarten, we should have blinked and smiled and said Leo, what are you talking about? He'd have been on the back foot straight away – "I have been told this, I've heard that…" "Well, we obviously discuss all sorts of things amongst ourselves, we're not idiots…" We could have put ourselves into a negotiating position, and things might have turned out a bit differently. I can construct, even now, in my mind the conversation that might have ensued; in fact, I can do it in Italian. Facts, rumours, innuendo, would've been bounced across the table, a very Italian style of negotiation – conducted on the visible surface of a deep iceberg – and at the end there would have been, not a handshake but at least the recognition that a future handshake wasn't yet ruled out: *"mi pare che forse esiste la possibilita di qualche gener di accomodazione…"* Straight out of The Godfather. But in fact we were idiots, rammed to our ears with arrogance, self-fuelled anger and hubris. Confrontation selected itself, there was no thought process, no strategy. And Roger's emotions were in charge.

Next day we were called to a meeting at Leo's office behind Corso Vittorio Emanuele II. We shouldn't have gone. If you're dumping someone who has more power than you – sacking your boss – the last thing to do is walk into his lair. It may have been Bob who persuaded us that this was necessary, that we owed an explanation or something to Leo.

The meeting wasn't a meeting. It was a vicious personal attack on me, one on one. I'd guess that I was singled out because he knew I was the best amongst us at Italian. Because of the previous night's scene at the Rosengarten, he probably also assumed that I was the hatcher and mastermind of this plot. Totally untrue, as usual I was just going along with the flow. The plot had been cooked up, by Roger and Alfio, without my involvement in any of the discussions – I certainly never spoke to anyone from Ricordi (around whom the whole thing was meant to revolve). In any case, I had no defence against the vilification. Leo cast me as a Nazi, a persecutor of Jews such as him.

I can't, and don't want to recall the details. All I could do was sit there and take it – we didn't have any kind of strategy or even position to oppose to this. The others could obviously sense what was going on, but didn't have the language to jump in and counter it. Braver or smarter people would've insisted on English, all talked at once and demanded translation: all the kinds of ploys I'd deploy if I was there again today, knowing what I know now; but as it was, we sat there, letting him take his high ground and grind me down under his boot heel, whilst everyone blushed and cringed.

At a certain point, I think Roger sensed that Leo had gone too far, stood up and said come on, we're walking out. Which we did. Except Bob. Bob did physically walk out with us, but sometime soon afterwards he walked out on us.

I have notes, which I made some time after the event, of those intense three days. They mean very little to me now, at least as a means to reconstructing the factual detail. I know that there was a go-between called Zilli, who I think worked for Ricordi, and that Alfio found us a lawyer (*avocato*) called Vallino, who expressed a top-of-his-head opinion that our contract with Pitt, and hence with Leo, was invalid under Italian law, but this would of course have to be tested through the Italian legal process. There were all sorts of other issues. Did we have a recording contract with SAAR? (Answer: no.) What about work/residence permits? I attended a meeting at the *Questura* with a Dr Paolella (at, it appears, 10.30 on Saturday, which seems unlikely); the *Dottore* advised that, as long as we had money to live on, we could stay in Italy, no problem.

One seemingly trivial aside in my notes reads as follows (this is on the same Saturday): 'Arango phoned – said Leo prepared to pay Ken if we go to Bologna. Checked with Vallino – doesn't make any difference to us whether Leo pays Ken or not.'

Looking at it now, I guess this was actually a tipping point. Leo, via Dr Arango as a presumably trusted intermediary, was extending a substantial olive branch, in fact more like a whole grove: Ken's share of our debt must have been well over half of the 25m lire. Leo must have been desperate. I don't know what 'Bologna' was, but it was obviously a symbolic gig. Vallino was absolutely right, from the contractual point of view – it didn't make any difference, insofar as we'd already made our decision. But it certainly should have done. It should certainly have been given more consideration. I think I raised it with Roger; but you can't conduct a rational consideration, from the perspective of financial risk/benefit, musical advancement or career prospects, with a besotted psychopath. So I didn't stand a chance. Maybe he didn't even hear me; maybe I didn't even really raise it properly. Who knows.

So now I'm torn at least three ways. Go forward with the Roger/Alfio scenario; crawl back to Leo; or try and get us back to England. The last was always my number one. I'd always thought, what's this great band, challengers to the greatest and best, doing hauling around two-bit gigs in this musically unconscious land?

At this point, it might be worth glancing at the Italian music scene as it was then, at what we were up against. The establishment was firmly rooted in Italian tradition, which in effect meant power ballads, preferably in minor keys, preferably sung by big-busted females like Ornella Vanoni or tuxedoed males. The way to make commercial or popular success was to participate in one of the many song festivals which took place over the summer season. San Remo was the biggie, but there were a few upstarts, less focussed on the star than on the music. Leo had sent us to the Rieti festival, up in the mountains behind Rome, dedicated to 'i complessi', groups, so some kind of 'alternative' event, where we apparently made a bit of an impression, winning something called the 'critics prize'; this was vaunted as a major breakthrough, but if so, we missed the point. Or the point missed us – we didn't want to break through to the traditional Italian music scene, we wanted Italy to break through to us. Obviously there was no shortage of support for this attitude, and the number of groups, both native and Brit expat, was growing by the day. But the establishment didn't have a clue what was going on.

These days, the breach with Leo having become a fait accompli more or less by default, most of our efforts had to be directed towards a) sorting out the contractual situation, and b) establishing some kind of income stream, i.e. getting gigs. The Equipe were meant to be helping with both of these. I've already talked about their efforts towards a), which consisted of handing us over to the mercies of the hardnosed (and as it turned out avaricious) lawyer Vallini. On the second front, the first gig Alfio found us was, we were assured, going to be a showcase. The plan was that DAM's visibility and saleability would be massively boosted in the Italian impresario marketplace by playing three or four nights at this hot spot nightclub in Rome, where all the important people fetched up.

The flaws in this plan are too obvious to recount. For a start, if we were so desirable, why did we need to put ourselves around? Surely they should be chasing us. Also, how could we be expected to present ourselves at our best in some unseen, seemingly very small pokehole in Rome, a city where we'd dismally failed in all our previous appearances? Our strong home ground was in the north, Milan, Piedmont, Reggio Emilia. If we really did need a relaunch of some kind, it should have been somewhere like the Santa Tecla in Milan, or one of the growing number of enthusiast cliques in small towns all over northern Italy. But we allowed ourselves to be convinced by Alfio's assurances that everybody that mattered would be there.

So we go to Rome (prudently retaining our rooms at Mama's pensione in Milan) and manage to find this nightclub, the name of which I'm glad to say I will never remember. Pokehole is right – the joint makes the Cromwellian seem cavernous. The stage is the size of a couple of sofas. There's no way two Marshall stacks will fit on there, so Bill and I have to reset our amps to work through a single speaker each, and balance these on top of each other. Even then there's only just room left for the organ and drums on the platform. Roger and the horns have to work on the dancefloor. Hearts sink and heads are shaken. When we do a run-through that afternoon, the proprietor rushes out in dismay: *"piu piano, piano*, quieter, quieter, *troppo forte!"*

He then informed us that we had to do something called a *'sigla'*, a seamless segue (which I think was the word he was looking for) between the recorded background music and the live performance. This guy reminded me strongly of Reg, the assassin of La Fiesta back in 1963 Southbourne. He demonstrated how this musical transition would work, with fluttering hands and hip-swaying body language. The background music was Italian cocktail sub-jazz, with wispy strings and brushed drums, so we got Bob to play *Blue Moon*, the only standard he knew, fading up on the Hammond's volume pedal as the record slush fades down. We would then kick in to our opening number, which was usually, still, *Walk On The Wild Side*.

Luckily we only had to do this once. The Roman impresarios had unaccountably stayed away. The few Romans who did show up mostly shouted at each other to drown out the noise. Ominous wisps of smoke rose from the back of my Marshall amp, in protest at only being allowed a single speaker cabinet to work with (or possibly at the amp-to-speaker cable not being properly connected – neither I nor the Marshall had ever tried this before, and hindsight insinuates that the thing never sounded quite as good afterwards). Roman Reg shimmered around the edges of the room, blowing 'ssh' gestures at us as we gamely whispered our way through *Hold On I'm Coming* and *Knock On Wood*. Memory, thankfully, edits out details, but I'm fairly sure that we were invited not to bother coming on for our second set. Next day, we crawled back to Milan, heads and tails low. Shortly afterwards Bob left the band.

I don't recall any conversations with him about his reasons for this. He's since told me that, in a word, he'd had enough – of the slogging around in the van, the drink, the other people's drugs; and, probably, the music. At the time, if I thought at all about it (and there really wasn't much of that going on), I reckon I put it down to some kind of misplaced or displaced loyalty – to Pitt, back through Wachter. My relationship with Bob had indeed deteriorated over the years: probably as my need for a friend diminished as the availability of the pool of friends expanded, I neglected him. Being the closed person he was, and the confused open person I thought I was, we wouldn't have talked about it.

Strangely, I don't think he actually did have any devious agenda. He wanted a quiet, simple life, playing his own music, living in a village somewhere. But deviousness, or presenting the front of deviousness, was the only tactic he possessed; and once that front had to face up against this hard wall between commitment and loyalty, he just decided to walk away, in whatever direction.

At the time, Bob's defection didn't seem to present any kind of major block to our callous ambition: we'll just have to get another organist, won't we? That was our callous thinking. And funnily enough, there's one available, Chris Dennis. Simplification hero to the rescue.

Chris had played with an English group called the Bad Boys, who we'd kind of met at the Piper back in March, and then shared support billing on the New Vaudeville Band tour. I'd got on well with their guitarist, Roger Dean, and traded licks with him – he was strong on the jazzy stuff, I was strong on blues. As I've said, I have a blind spot when it comes to playing jazz; I can often hear it in my head, but getting that to my fingers is another matter entirely. Partly it's to do with speed – my right hand guitar technique has never been adept enough for the precise picking required to keep up with the left; also, my left hand doesn't really know where it's going either. Well, that just about sums up my jazz guitar capabilities. So, through no fault of his own, I guess Roger Dean probably got more than I did out of those exchanges. After all, playing blues is dead easy. (Playing it well, not quite so.)

Anyway, there was a quick-fire transition. The Bad Boys had broken up and Chris had gone back to England, tail between his legs, repatriated via the British Consulate. We got in touch with him, by letter – so addresses must have been exchanged at some point, neither of us can quite remember the details – but he responded to the summons. I can only quote his words:

"Off the top of my head I remember receiving *the call* in late autumn or early winter. I remember walking from the main station to (perhaps) the Rosengarten to meet up with someone, but on the other hand I might have walked all the way to 'Mama's'. Whatever, it was a long way. It was incredibly warm compared with England. I had my cardboard suitcase (after all, and even if I didn't know it at the time, I was *emigrating*) and was wearing a heavy overcoat: by the time I arrived I was drenched in sweat." I don't remember it quite like that, obviously.

We must have installed Chris in a spare bed at Mama's, and undertaken some kind of fast-track rehearsal process. He knew most of our increasingly stale repertoire, and I guess we might have dropped some of the more intricately arranged numbers, like *Walk On The Wild Side*, at this point – in other words the material that had given Dave Anthony's Moods, back in 1966, what's now called its 'unique selling point', that combination of power brass and slick precisely delivered scoring that had led the well-meaning Chris Welch, in the Melody Maker, to compare us to the great Big Bands of an earlier era. From now on, we'd be a slick, professional gigging outfit with absolutely no musical focus. Although no-one would've admitted it, at this point the dream, such as it had ever been, was over.

Let me say at once that this shift in the band's paradigm was in no way the fault of Chris, or Bob, or anyone else, except perhaps me. The time of jazzy r'n'b was gone forever. Back in England, Georgie Fame had gone pop, whilst Zoot Money (perhaps with his tongue hovering around one of his chubby cheeks) had transmogrified into Dantaleon's Chariot, complete with druid robes and firecrackers. James Brown hadn't yet quite invented funk, and Sly was some way in the future, at least in Italy. For a band like ours, there was nowhere obvious to go, but no shortage of possible directions. A glance at some of the records we were listening to demonstrates this: *Are You Experienced?*, *Piper At The Gates Of Dawn*, *Mr Fantasy*, *Vanilla Fudge*, *The Crazy World Of Arthur Brown*, *Smiley Smile*, something embarrassing by Donovan... I don't need to go on. The diversity, even within any one of those albums, is bewildering now – none of them would pass the style censors today. I suppose at the time, though, this all must have seemed like a single direction – a new one! – (although some of the increasingly far out jazz stuff (Coltrane, Dolphy), plus a few inexplicable items from the classical world (Berg) lurked on the sidelines); but whether or not it was really a single direction, albeit a streaky, whizzy unfocussed polychromatic one, it most definitely didn't point anywhere, either back or forwards.

We had of course been experimenting ever since Roger joined us – remember the short-lived flirtation with stage make-up. He and Bob had been unlikely allies in this; Roger loved theatricals, and Bob loved anything that was unlike anything else. We once spent a whole day, at the Piper Torino, developing and rehearsing a kind of performance art happening, complete with imagined costumes, ritual murders and I forget what else, which fell apart when it became evident that we didn't have any actual music to go with it. So the trend in late 67 towards the freak-out rather than the dance set didn't meet with much resistance within DAM, especially once you add in the drugs. Bob was the only one who didn't add them in, and once he left we were, for a long time, a bunch of seriously committed potheads.

I now know that drugs don't enhance the creative process, but do, for certain classes of musician, assist with the performance. I need to qualify that. By the creative process, I mean the concentrated mental and physical effort, often very boring, which results in a performable construct in real time. You can't do that when you're stoned. Our original arrangement of *Walk On The Wild Side*, for example, would never have happened if John, Graham and I had been zonked when we developed it back there in Hutchings Walk. Secondly, when I talk about the performance, and about 'certain classes', it's a fact that the more physical effort required, the less the dope will help. That's why so many drummers burn out. Certainly it's why ours did.

• • •

After the Roman fiasco things seemed to settle down for a while. We got some gigs, mostly via our own efforts using contacts supposedly provided by the Equipe. And Ricordi seemed to be enthusiastic. A young producer, whose name I've forgotten if I ever knew it, was put onto our case. One day, he told us that Lucio Battisti, together with his adventurous lyricist Mogol, had come up with a song that might suit us. Battisti, who subsequently became a bit of a superstar, was at this time an aspirant songwriter who had yet to realise his potential as a singer, and so he and Mogol were churning out potboilers for anyone who was prepared to listen. We were given a demo of a song called *La Fossa degli Serpenti, The Snakepit*. It was a complex, not to say convoluted, story in which the said pit was equated both to a sleazy nightclub and to the turmoil in the singer's mind.

I loved it, both for its lyrical ambiguities and for the tightly segmented musical structure, which made *Good Vibrations* look simplistic. Over-enthusiastically, I sketched out an arrangement in my notebook, complete with instructions as to how it should be mixed, how much of what kind of echo should be applied to particular instruments and chords, and when mandolins, harpsichords and heavenly choirs should come in. What's the word for an aural vision? Whatever it is, I clearly had one of those in my head when I wrote that. Just a sample, literally transcribed: '... voices – subdued. Much echo. D chord – bring vocal up. Weird bit – voices minus echo. Build-up – drums/bass reinforce in last phrase of verse then 5 changes of chords 1 add mandogtr + harpsichord 2 brass chords build (gets more complicated 3 high echo voices 4 fade in dong dong ?cowbell 5 brass < everything else...'

I'd love to hear that! And I probably could, if I could only remember the song. I still get a lot of those auro-visions. I sometimes wake up with them in my ears, and wish myself back to sleep.

It wasn't much like that when we went into the Ricordi studio to cut the record. The intro section of the song called for a two-chord jam invoking the atmosphere of the snakepit club, which would fade into the singer's introspective first verse. It was meant to be wild, fuzzy, dangerous. I had to deliver this, at nine in the morning, with my newly acquired wah-wah pedal, no fuzz, no danger. Bill and John were to say the least noncommittal. As we were plodding away, two things happened – Andy suggested we all nipped out to the gents, and Battisti walked through the door, carrying his twelve string. He was all charm, big smiles, big Italian afro hair. We'd got back from the gents in the meantime. Lucio basically took over the production: he let us finish the snakepit intro jam, which was, it seemed, much better this time round, then suggested, in effect, that he lay down a guide track on guitar, which we could all play along to afterwards. I think he probably did a guide vocal too – why he didn't just release it under his own name, as was, I don't know, because I remember it as a coruscating solo performance; you knew you were in the presence of star quality. But instead, we built our own competent rhythm track, dubbed on a punchy brass arrangement (with which I had nothing to do, I guess I was sulking because my psychedelic bell-laden aural vision had quite rightly been dumped, or just politely ignored), and a few days later Roger was induced to overdub a passable vocal, in Italian, on Ricordi's newly acquired eight-track recorder. For the B side we dashed off a weird Bee Gees number called *Jumbo*, about which I remember nothing.

Then it all went quiet. We continued to get work, but it became increasingly clear that the Equipe weren't really engaged. They'd given us a few contacts, sure, but from then on it was all down to us. Similarly the relationship with Ricordi became more remote once the sessions had finished. I want to spend some time on this latter aspect, because it came back to haunt us. So I'm going to apply lashings of hindsight and guesswork, to arrive at the following reconstruction.

Ricordi bought the remnants of the Ken Pitt contract from Leo Wachter. This was, however, a purely financial accommodation, which didn't carry with it any artistic or managerial commitment. Why did they do this? I think that Alfio was genuinely enthused by DAM, or at least by Roger, and the Equipe were a powerful force, driving a wedge into the monolithic Italian music establishment, of which I've already written. My guess is that Ricordi was at this time a classic traditionally structured business, with many deep layers of management and authority, within which a swell of turbulence was bubbling up – just like EMI in England really. The business models (not that anyone thought in such terms: the expression would have met with bemused incomprehension in both

London and Milan) were crumbling and cracking. So it would have been possible for Alfio to gain the ear of some currently significant mid-layer enthusiast and convince him that the company should take on and assist this brilliant but struggling band. All it'd take would be to pay off a few debts (amounts not specified of course) and make a record. And so it came to pass. This much, so far, isn't really in dispute.

Next, there would have been the misunderstanding about how we'd actually make our money, day to day – food, drink, transport, drugs. In quite a short time we'd got used to the salaried scheme, where Leo paid us our monthly wage regardless of what we were, or very often weren't doing. (Come to think of it, had he assumed that this covered earnings from record sales as well as gigs? It would certainly explain why to this day I don't know how many copies were sold of the two Italian singles.) Anyway, I think that we supposed that there was some kind of work guarantee, or at least assurance, in there; whereas in fact once we became (sort of) free from the Pitt-Leo contract, we were basically on our own. I certainly didn't understand any of this at the time.

So there was a dichotomy between what we (or I) thought we were getting from the Equipe/Ricordi axis and what they thought they were giving us. As I say, confusion across the piece. There's evidence that, at this time, Ricordi were issuing publicity posters. If I'm right, then the one unanswered question has to be: why didn't they release the record?

Rumours persist on the internet that *Jumbo* exists on a mythical RCA Italia compilation, but nobody has ever physically tracked it down. As for the A side, the Battisti song, there's no trace (he re-used the concept for a later song called *La Fossa dei Leoni*). My personal recollection is that it was pretty damn good

– a punchy performance, a state-of-the-art recording (eight tracks, for God's sake!) and a pioneering song. If I'm right, it wasn't rejected on grounds of quality. Nor can it have been down to commercial considerations: at that time, anything slightly different would sell enough to recoup its costs, and DAM were actually pretty popular in Italy. So it must have been down to intrigue.

It seems extraordinary now to think that groups, or their backers, would be terrified, to the extent of committing or sanctioning sabotage, of a rival group putting out a record, but that seems to be what happened. In short, I believe that the Equipe chopped us off because they were jealous and afraid. That they had to go to such lengths, and do it in such an incompetent and unfeeling manner, says as much as anything else about the pervasively destructive influence of drugs. Meanwhile, Dave Anthony's Moods were cut loose without knowing it yet, like a failing swimmer who still trusts in his deflating water wings.

• • •

Musically, we were both tight and loose. Tight, because by now we'd been playing together long enough to function, at our best and on tried and tested material, as a single unit on stage. Chris imposed some much needed discipline in this area: he'd played with some pretty formidable soulsters, and I remember very clearly one drugged-out evening when he conveyed to me the following profound musical insight: you need to be able to count to four, at a constant speed. I think that idea switched on my internal metronome – it seems blindingly obvious now, and clearly I wasn't unaware of the concept of tempo, but maybe until then I'd never quite placed it at the centre of performance.

At any rate, I know that my notebooks show that I started to chop up the eighths, sixteenths or even thirty-secondths of a bar of four-four, sticking in harsh pencil arrows at beat 19/32 where an essential stress had to fall... Obsessively dope-induced, of course; but this may have been some kind of cusp for me. Certainly, at our best, on stage, for perhaps the first time, we grooved.

Loose, because – well, I've pretty much covered this ground. If we'd had any semblance of management as the role is now understood, we'd have been picked up by the scruffs of our necks, shaken around and dropped on the individual sixpences of our assigned jobs. We were indeed a well-oiled machine, but one that hadn't been designed to do anything in particular. Heath Robinson meets the Vogons. This mythical manager, let's call him Simon Epstein, would have picked out Andy as the upfront charisma star, me as the musical brain, Bill as the prime sex appeal, Chris as the cheeky one... then selected a single musical route and forced us down it to the exclusion of all else. We wouldn't have been allowed to tinker with puerile imitations of Traffic B-sides or Vanilla Fudge harmonies or folksy whimsy (*So Sad*) or Sub-Continental freakouts (*See My Soul*). I'd have been disciplined to write or arrange only within the parameters of this defined, agreed musical direction, instead of flying off all over the place and producing stuff that there was no chance of DAM ever performing. Roger would probably have been sacked. John might have survived.

John had been falling apart, gradually, ever since we went to Italy. In Via Lamarmora, in the thick intrigues and alliances, very often I think he was the most whispered against. And a disintegrating person can't integrate. He took refuge in introspective drinking, which didn't go down well, for two reasons. Firstly, the rest of us were tiptoeing or being sucked towards that sanctimonious late sixties sub-genre of hippydom which eschewed adrenaline- and alcohol-fired excess in favour of wafty, flowery pot-smoothed vegetarian tweeness: the same progression that musicians like Stevie Winwood made, in his case from *I'm a Man* to Traffic's more flutey efforts like *Hole In My Shoe*. So boozy rampages were, for the most part, out of fashion in six-sevenths of the band (though Roger and I would still be up for it on occasions), and continuous reliance on drink to boost performance or get you through the day wasn't in the frame. Secondly, of course, constantly pissed drummers can't keep time. So we couldn't count on the groove.

We were still pretty good though, good enough to get enough work to survive. This despite an extent of multi-tasking that would be inconceivable to the most humble of today's bands. Consider: in addition to the core business of getting up on stage and playing the music well enough to, at least, get paid, and even better get rebooked, between us we still had to perform all those roles that today are, I'm sure, taken for granted as being someone else's job. Manager. Booking agent. Road manager. Driver. Equipment humper. Sound engineer. Technician. I could expand and continue the list for a page. Catering. Drug procurement. Counselling…

Of course, most of these didn't really exist as discernable positions. They were just part of the whole thing, stuff we'd more or less taken for granted since 1964; in this sense, the Leo episode was an exception, a brief flash of luxurious freedom (which, as I've noted, we completely wasted). 'Manager' wasn't really a consideration; we were past the stage of needing image creation or media manipulation, and capital investment was a sour joke in our situation. 'Booking agent' was another matter:

we needed to get gigs. A kind of deal was struck whereby Roger and I would perform this role, sharing a ten percent 'commission' on the proceeds. I can't imagine why I agreed to this, as hustling had (and has) never been one of my inclinations or skills. But gigs were nevertheless obtained. When it came to share-out time, just before Christmas 1967, the Roger-driven consensus was that I'd hardly contributed anything to this and thus wouldn't receive my share. This was entirely fair and justified, by the rules that had been set; but I'd been counting on that money, and resented what I saw as an act of theft. I felt that the reason I hadn't contributed was that I hadn't been allowed to. Meetings, contacts, agreements were going on behind my back. On the odd occasion when I tried to join in, I felt sidelined.

There were some contacts, so we got gigs. I remember three from that period.

The first was in a small town in Emilia, a drill hall job, where we played a truncated version of the usual set then spent half an hour on an extended *Shotgun*. I've already told how this number had, back in England, been stretched, but by now it had evolved into an improvisatory showpiece. We would do the song, as per the record; then I'd start a solo. Then all hell would break loose. Although I was a fairly competent blues hacker, there was no way I could have sustained a Santana-type extended blast to hold an audience enthralled on my own; so it evolved into a group jam. That doesn't mean half an hour of everyone hammering away at once, oh no. I'd do my obligatory fast-fingered sixteen bars, then we'd take it down and make eye contact. After that, anything might happen. John, actually, was great in these scenarios, because he didn't have to obey the laws of strict tempo but could play around with little tinkles on the bells of his cymbals… Chris revelled in picking out those odd harmonics that others could zing off… and Andy and Graham just wandered off into their own louvered room (one eye open for when someone – anyone really – might raise the head and tip the wink that, OK, enough maybe?)… Meanwhile, I'd be sparking off little tunes which might, if lucky, send the whole thing off in yet another direction…

Usually, this indulgent stuff would turn off the audience fairly quickly, and we'd have the nous to realise that and move on. But that particular gig is here in my vision, that community hall, I even imagine I can picture the faces of the boys and girls, urging us on, and on, and on…

The second one is down in Genoa. Late nights are wasted in dangerous waterfront bars, where sailors drink and hookers hunt. I go through one of those three-hour pissed love affairs with an irresistible, instantly forgettable short-haired girl … We live in some kind of pensione at the bottom of a tower block, and one night take the lift up to the twenty-fourth floor, lean over a low balcony in order to stare down the liftwell, a vertigo dare… After the end of the three-night gig, the proprietor apologetically tells me that he hasn't broken even, so he can't pay us our promised basic wage… I remember Tony at the Disque in Bournemouth and refuse to shake this man's proffered hand. This bit of quixotry turns out to cost us a lot of bookings. Idiot me? Yes, but principled me as well.

Any principles vanish, dissolved in shame, in my third memory, a small-scale gig in what I remember as a school hall, though it can't have been. They were kind and welcoming, so I chose to steal from them – two packs of foolscap paper from their stationery cupboard, in an office they'd allowed us to use as a dressing room. I got caught, but somehow covered up the theft. I have a vivid memory of it – the head guy chasing me out of the building, accusing me of stealing a towel (I had, the paper was hidden under the stolen towel)… A week or two later, they conducted an inventory which proved that this dumb low-value larceny had indeed taken place. That probably cost us a few gigs as well. Shameful.

So we staggered on down the crumbling track we'd set ourselves on, or been steered onto. Everyone knew there was something wrong. We were working, but it was diminishing. We half-heartedly rehearsed a few new numbers – pretty competent DAM horn-based takes on Vanilla Fudge's revolutionary takes on Motown, one or two ballads that had caught my or Roger's ears – but there was no direction any more. In addition to Pitt and Leo, it now seemed that we owed money to Ricordi as well.

• • •

One day, out of nowhere, a kind of weak salvation appeared. Leo managed a singer called Maurizio Arcieri, who'd formerly had some success with a group called the New Dada, but had gone solo and scored a massive hit with a good song called *Cinque Minuti e Poi – Five Minutes and Then*. It was the summer hit – Disco per l'Estate – of 1968. As I've already explained, the Italian pop scene at the time was driven by contests and festivals, and winning one of these required immediate cash-in. Maurizio didn't have a group, having alienated most of his previous collaborators, and Leo saw a two-bird one-stone opportunity. Dave Anthony's Moods would back Maurizio on his summer tour. The deal was that the Moods would play their own half-hour set as warm-up band, then Maurizio would come on and do his star turn, culminating in *Cinque Minuti*. It was never written down, but the nudge-wink understanding was that our debt to Leo, and thence to Ken Pitt, would become quietly forgotten. As would the debt to Ricordi.

That regime lasted for a few weeks, but it wasn't enough for Leo, or for Maurizio, or indeed for us. There was a lot of sneaky snaky wriggling. Relations within the band hit rock bottom. Roger and I were barely speaking. Bill was having underhand discussions, it seemed, with shadowy figures about forming some kind of Italian supergroup. Remember what was going on in England at the same time. Cream and Traffic had dissolved into Blind Faith, Led Zeppelin were coming through on the outside. The Beatles had dissipated into three solo stars, each with his own backing group (but the same drummer) and back-up teams. 'The Beatles' double LP was in gestation in studios all over the hemisphere whilst Paul's magical mystery vanity trip was leaving us all a bit perplexed... Nobody had a clue what was going on. In this feverish atmosphere, filtered through and intensified by the mist of distance, no wonder that our broken-down band was floundering about like a beached flatfish.

Over a cocktail of amphetamines, hash, whisky and suppressed sex, in a bar in Torino, the deal was struck. The intricacies are lost to time now but the outcome was a simple one, in which I was at the least complicit, if not exigent. In fact, I take the blame. I'd had enough of Roger: his duplicity, his bullying, his failure. I'd also had enough of playing *Night Train* and *Loving You Too Long*, going through the motions. In that bar in Torino, sitting there with Maurizio hopped up out of our heads, we thrashed out a repertoire which, we convinced ourselves, would be a rebirth. All the old songs would be junked, instead we'd be slicing at the cutting edge. My memory, mercifully, fails at the details – I know we had to do one or two Italian songs, I got a guitar feature (Hendrix's *Manic Depression*) we picked up a bit of Blood Sweat and Tears. The latter in particular interested me, as a possible route back to the jazzy big band sound we'd started from back in Bournemouth. I'd also started to hear Sly and the Family Stone, and James Brown's second incarnation – punchy, brassy, riff-driven, hardly any chords, certainly none of the folksy druggy-hippy indulgence I'd been so besotted with a few long months before. Here, I thought, might be a way back to a way forward. Recovery, repair and restitution.

Meanwhile, we had to sack Roger, and secure Bill. I have several pages of scrawled notes, written over an intensive three-day period which must have been ram packed with intrigue and third party negotiation, about how this could be achieved. How much of this actually happened I have no idea, and it doesn't matter. For now, at least, the money had spoken. Six months previously, we'd turned up at the Milan Piper in the hope of seeing Procol Harum, and got seen off with giant fleas in our ears by a Leo looming behind a squad of heavies. This time, it was Jimi Hendrix. Leo now gave warm handshakes, waved away our money, and welcomed us.

After

So that's the end of Dave Anthony's Moods.

Roger left to join the Primitives. Bill stayed.

As Maurizio's backing group, we went on the road, efficiently commuting from gig to gig, for eighteen-plus months. We got a slick new van, another Transit, this one with side windows and proper seats, to replace old Bessie who had finally sighed and said 'enough', after about 100,000 miles. And a slick new roadie, Davide. We worked up some slick new material: an enhanced take on Paul and Barry Ryan's *Eloise*, and a minor hit by I forget who, a medley of *I Can Sing a Rainbow* and *Love Is Blue*; I loved both of these, they stretched my arranging and composing abilities once again, climbing on the back of Jim Webb's adventurous, operatic experiments with Richard Harris and the Fifth Dimension. (In fact it's fair to say that I was far more interested in writing than in performing by now.) I was persuaded to retain my *Manic Depression* guitar feature, becoming increasingly embarrassed at having to go through the motions.

I can't pretend I didn't enjoy a lot of it. I can remember many events and places and incidents, which I could probably make another chapter out of if I chose to; but this is about Dave Anthony's Moods, and Dave Anthony's Moods was over. Oh, all right, just the one. (I did promise it earlier on.)

After

Three of us – me John and Graham – were driving a rented van from Milan to Rome, the others for some reason having gone on ahead. Also for some reason, I was carrying Andy's documents, including his International Driving Licence. John had packed in the pot by then, and was driving; but Graham and I were well advanced by the time the traffic police pulled us over somewhere near Florence. John produced his IDL, but then, in a moment of possibly misplaced honesty, pointed out that it had expired, actually. The *polizie* were not amused. "Follow us," they ordered. Graham and I exchanged an apprehensive glance. I seem to remember that we might have lingered in Milan in order to collect a significant score; we were equipped for a serious legal run-in. My own IDL had also expired, but in a flash of inspiration I remembered that Andy's hadn't. IDLs didn't contain a photograph. I took a deep breath and showed it to the cops. They broke into big grins, reminding me of the border guards at the top of the Mont Blanc tunnel when we'd first entered Italy all those centuries ago. They were obviously relieved at this get-out. *"Guida lei!"* they cried, "You drive!" So I did.

And then there were the Calabrian hill towns, where the police patrolled in pairs, with dogs, and black-clad women in doorways hid their children behind their skirts as we walked past; Paola, balanced atop a vertical cliff five hundred metres above the cold black waters of the Gulf of Taranto, where the baker's son made us get up at five to taste the best hot bread in the universe; Lecce, an oasis of enlightenment ("They're Arabs", a student explained to me, gesturing towards Calabria; "We're Greeks."); riding the white surf at Viareggio with two beautiful, innocent sisters… I'm sorry, I said I wouldn't do this, so I'd better stop now.

John finally broke down, and had to be sent home. I still don't know what happened to his Ludwigs and Ziljians. The replacement drummer, Gualtiero, was a jazzy technician, totally unsuited, arrogant and even worse at strict tempo. Everyone recognised that we had to go home, or move on. Break up. Bill and I sold our Marshall amps to an aspirant group somewhere down in the Mezzogiorno, to raise enough cash to repatriate ourselves.

When we played the last tired gig, somewhere near Modena, with borrowed amplifiers, a DAM fan from way back came up to me afterwards and asked, sadly and anxiously: *"Ma – cos'e successo?"* "But – what happened?"

What Happened?

The last I heard:

Bob Michaels stayed in Italy. He played with a few bands, then fetched up as the organist and choirmaster of a church in Lugano, just over the border in Switzerland, where he still officiates, and is a leading light in the world of European choristry.

Bill Jacobs emigrated to Australia and went into software development. He's recently got back into making music. He claims that he never wanted to be a bass player.

Andy Kirk returned to England, became a farmer, played in local Dorset bands and raised a family, before turning back into the loner he always was. He now lives in France and globe trots.

Graham Livermore returned to Poole, where he fell back into local jazz gigs but eventually gave up active music making. He died in October 2013.

John Devekey, I understand, is well and living in Bournemouth.

Pete Sweet returned to managing his Southbourne hotel, and gigged regularly with Graham on the local jazz circuit. His health deteriorated, and he died in 2001.

What Happened

Tony Head (Dave Anthony) went on to some success with Tony and Tandy and the Fleur de Lys. He died in 2006.

Roger Peacock eventually became a beach bum in Goa, where he died in a freak motorcycle accident.

Bob Downes went on to a successful career in the avant garde jazz world, and now lives in Germany.

Chris Dennis stayed on in Italy, where he is still musically active as a performer and teacher, and translates patents.

Ken Pitt is, as far as I can tell, still around at 90-plus.

Leo Wachter died in 2000.

Maurizio Arcieri continued to perform, going through a punk phase in the seventies. He died in 2015.

Tim Large returned to England, where he swerved into a fairly successful career in banking IT and retired in 2000. He's now sitting here writing this.